The Official
THEORY TEST
for Learner Drivers
in all Licence Categories

G000122961

Questions and Answers

Written and compiled by the Department of the Environment and Local Government

Acknowledgements

The Department of the Environment and Local Government would like to thank the following for their assistance:

National Roads Authority

National Safety Council

An Garda Síochána

The Department of Education and Science

The Association for Children and Adults with Learning Disabilities

The National Adult Literacy Agency

Staff of the Department of the Environment and Local Government

Every effort has been made to ensure that at the time of printing the information contained in this book is accurate. Information in this book is for guidance only and is not an interpretation of the law.

Foreword

It is important that learner drivers have a knowledge of the principles of safe driving as well as the practical ability to drive competently and responsibly. The introduction of a theory test to ensure learner drivers have a good understanding of the driving environment is an important step towards improving road safety in this country.

The driver theory test is designed to help you to be a safe, courteous and informed driver. It is relevant to your preparation as a driver whether you are a young learner driver being tested on road signs, attitudes to other road users, or driving risks; or an aspiring professional truck or bus driver being tested on such matters as braking systems, use of the tachograph, or load distribution.

This book, along with the Rules of the Road will help you prepare for your theory test and ultimately for your driving career. The questions are set out in an easy to read style with the correct answers identified.

Introduction

Driver Theory Test

The driving theory test is designed to examine the driving knowledge of novice drivers. There are three separate theory tests dependent on the vehicle categories which the person wishes to have on their provisional licence or driving licence. These are set out in the following table:

Theory Test Certificate Category	Driving Licence / Provisional Licence category
A, B, M and W	A, A1, B, EB, M and W
C	C, C1, EC and EC1
D	D, D1, ED and ED1

This book contains the theory test question bank for each licence category.

The following table provides details of the vehicles covered by each driving licence category:

CATEGORY

A	motorcycles	

A1	motorcycles with an engine capacity not exceeding 125 cubic centimetres and with a power rating not exceeding 11 kilowatts	

B	cars (and other vehicles) having a design gross weight not exceeding 3,500 kg. and having passenger accommodation for 8 (or fewer) persons. (Motorcycles, mopeds, work vehicles and land tractors are not included)	

C	trucks (or other vehicles) having a design gross weight exceeding 3,500 kg. and having passenger accommodation for 8 (or fewer) persons. (Work vehicles and land tractors are not included)	

C1	(trucks or other vehicles) in C having a design gross weight not exceeding 7,500 kg.	

D	buses having passenger accommodation for more than 8 persons	

D1	buses in D having accommodation for not more than 16 persons	

M	mopeds	

W	work vehicles and land tractors	

The tests for categories B, C, C1, D, D1 and W also cover provisional licences for these categories with a drawing vehicle without having to undergo a separate theory test.

Preparation

Make sure you are well prepared before applying for your test. Study carefully the material in this booklet in conjunction with the Rules of the Road booklet.

You should apply for a theory test to the Driver Theory Testing Service. The LoCall telephone number for the service is 1890 606106 for English language and 1890 606806 for Irish language. They will be able to give information as to where and when theory tests are held.

If you have special needs please state this on your application form so that appropriate arrangements may be made.

About this Book

Chapter 1 contains the questions which relate to the theory tests for categories A, B, M and W. These are the entry level licence categories i.e motorcycles, cars, mopeds, tractors and work vehicles.

Chapter 2, which has three parts, covers the progressive licence categories i.e. heavy goods vehicles and buses. Part 1 has questions common to both categories C and D; Part 2 has further questions solely for category C and Part 3 has further questions solely for category D. The theory test for these categories will also include questions from Chapter 1.

There are 3 answers per question and the correct (or most correct) answer for each question is marked with an asterisk.

Different types of questions are used:

- some questions show a picture or graphic of a traffic sign, road markings, traffic lights or hand signals with a question about interpretation.

For example:-

Q.   What does this sign mean?

Ans. (a)   One way street ahead.

        (b)   Parking permitted from this point on.

*   (c)   Straight ahead only.

- other questions are in words only where a question is posed or where a statement must be completed.

Examples are:

Q.   What should you do if the wipers are frozen to the windscreen?

Ans.   (a)   Switch the wipers to high speed to free them.

*   (b)   Defrost the windscreen before switching on the wipers.

    (c)   Pull the wipers free before switching them on.

Q. **A continuous vibration in the steering wheel while driving could indicate that .....**

Ans. * (a) the wheel balance is uneven
(b) the shock absorbers are worn
(c) weight distribution is uneven

Number of questions per test

Each test will comprise 40 questions.

If you have spent ample time and effort in preparing, you will not find the theory test difficult and you should pass the test. Then, when driving you can put the knowledge which you have gained into practice.

Contents

Forward   ii

Introduction   iii

Chapter 1
Categories A, B, M and W

Road Signs, Markings and Traffic Regulations   1

Regulatory Signs   1

Warning Signs   14

Motorway Signs   27

Road Signs   28

Hand Signals   34

Garda Signals   38

Road Markings   40

Traffic Lights   46

Speed Limits   49

Other Regulatory Matters   51

Alert Driving, and Consideration for Road Users   56

Anticipation   56

Consideration   58

Alertness   62

Observation/Field of View   64

Visibility   64

Blindspots   68

Reversing   70

Overtaking   71

U-turn   71

Good Judgement, and Perception   73

Fatigue   73

Awareness   74

Reaction Time   80

Attention   80

Patience   81

Alcohol   83

Medication   83

Observation of Safe Distance and Driving in
Various Weather/Road Conditions   84

Safe Distance/Clearance   84

Roadholding   87

Stopping Distance and Braking Ability   90

Driving Risk Factors Related to Various Road Conditions,
in Particular as They Change With the Weather and Time
of Day or Night   94

Driving in Fog   94

Driving at Night   95

Driving on Slippery Surfaces   101

Driving on a Flooded Road   103

Driving in Windy Conditions   104

Roadworks   105

Hump-Backed Bridge   105

Characteristics of Various Types of Road   106

One-way street   106

Bus lane   106

Dual-Carriageway   108

Motorway   109

Roads of Equal Importance   113

Clearway   113

Facing Downhill   114

Unmarked Road   114

Narrow Road   114

Roundabouts   115

Turning Right   117

Vulnerable Road Users   118

Allowing sufficient time for others   118

Reducing Speed having regard to other road users   121

Clearance   122

Anticipation of vulnerable road users   123

Signalling to Other Drivers   126

Necessary Documents   128

Driving Licence and Provisional Driving Licence Matters   128

Vehicle Registration and Tax Requirements   134

Insurance   136

Automatic Transmission   139

Accidents   140

What Action to Take   140

Collision – No Injury   141

Collision – Person Injured   141

Exchange of Information   144

Hazardous Materials   145

Safety Factors relating to Vehicle Loading and Persons Carried   146

Child Passengers   146

Carrying of Passenger   146

Children Driving   147

Effect of Impact on Passengers   147

Carrying a Passenger on a Motorcycle   148

Severe Braking   150

Safety   150

Load Carrying Capacity   150

Load Distribution   152

Position When Cornering   153

Trailers   154

Vehicle Handling   155

Technical Matters, with a Bearing on Road Safety   157

Headlights   157

Sidelights   158

Brake Lights   159

Warning Lights   159

Reflectors   161

Indicators   162

Brakes   162

Automatic Transmission   164

Vehicle Condition (Engine)   165

Fuel   165

Body Condition   165

Battery   166

Shock Absorbers/Suspension   166

Mirrors   166

Exhaust   167

Tyres   168

Clutch   172

Steering   173

Seat   173

Wipers   174

Windscreen   175

Environmental Matters	176
Fuel Consumption	176
Smoke	177
Noise	178
Horn	179
Getting Out From, or Off, the Vehicle	180
Vehicle Safety Equipment	183
Seat-belts	183
Children's Safety Seats	184
Side Impact Protection Bars	186

Chapter 2
Part 1
Categories C and D

Necessary Documents	187
Driving Hours and Rest Periods	188
Vehicle Weights and Dimensions	191
Braking Systems	192
Technical Matters with a bearing on road safety	195

Air Turbulence   197

Weather Related Matters   199

Driving Large or High-Sided Vehicles   202

Restricted Vision   205

Safety of Vehicle Loading and Persons Carried   207

Getting Out from the Vehicle   207

Accidents   209

Environmental Matters   209

Part 2
Categories C

Necessary Documents   211

Speed Limit   213

Vehicle Weights and Dimensions   213

Braking Systems   215

Technical Matters with a bearing on road safety   216

Safety of Vehicle Loading   217

Vehicle Safety Equipment   222

Getting out from the Vehicle   222

Environmental Matters   223

Part 3
Categories D

Necessary Documents   224

Speed Limit   225

Vehicle Weights and Dimensions   225

Braking Systems   226

Weather Related Matters   227

Carrying Passengers   227

Safety of Vehicle Loading   228

Vehicle Safety Equipment   229

Getting out from the vehicle   229

Accidents   230

Chapter 1

CATEGORIES A, B, M AND W

ROAD SIGNS, MARKINGS AND TRAFFIC REGULATIONS

REGULATORY SIGNS

Q. **What does this sign mean?**

Ans.

   (a)   Give way to traffic coming from your right.

   (b)   Other traffic must give way to you.

* (c)   Stop your vehicle

Q. **Where this sign is accompanied by a white stop line on the road, you should .....**

Ans.

   (a)   stop, when having passed the line.

* (b)   stop, in advance of the line.

   (c)   stop, only if there is traffic on the major road.

Q. Where this sign is not accompanied by a white line on the road, you should .....

Ans.
    (a) stop, only when having passed the sign.
* (b) stop in advance of the sign.
    (c) stop, only if there is traffic at the junction.

Q. What does this sign mean?

Ans.
    (a) Yield to buses only.
* (b) Yield to traffic on the major road.
    (c) Slow down and stop for pedestrians.

Q. What does this sign mean?

Ans.
    (a) No entry.
    (b) Yield to traffic coming from the right.
* (c) Yield to traffic on the major road.

Q. What does this sign mean?

Ans.
    (a) One way street ahead.
    (b) Parking permitted from this point on.
* (c) Straight ahead only.

Q.　　**What does this sign mean?**

Ans.　*　(a)　Turn left only.
　　　　　(b)　Motorway to the left.
　　　　　(c)　Traffic emerging from the
　　　　　　　right has priority.

Q.　　**What does this sign mean?**

Ans.　　(a)　Overtake only on the right.
　　　*　(b)　Turn right only.
　　　　　(c)　Major road joining from the
　　　　　　　left.

Q.　　**What does this sign mean?**

Ans.　　(a)　Diversion to the left ahead.
　　　　　(b)　Parking area to the left
　　　　　　　ahead.
　　　*　(c)　Turn left ahead.

Q.　　**What does this sign mean?**

Ans.　　(a)　Diversion to the right ahead.
　　　*　(b)　Turn right ahead.
　　　　　(c)　Sharp bend ahead.

Q.　　**What does this sign mean?**

Ans.　*　(a)　Keep left.
　　　　　(b)　Roundabout ahead.
　　　　　(c)　Sharp bend to the left
　　　　　　　ahead.

Q. **What does this sign mean?**

Ans. * (a) Keep right.
      (b) You must turn back.
      (c) Traffic crossing from the left.

Q. **What does this sign mean?**

Ans. (a) One-way street.
      (b) Dual-carriageway ahead.
* (c) Pass either side.

Q. **What does this sign mean?**

Ans. (a) Cul-de-sac ahead.
      (b) Parking not allowed up ahead.
* (c) No entry.

Q. **What does this sign mean?**

Ans. * (a) No right turn.
      (b) Turn right if there is no oncoming traffic.
      (c) Yield to other traffic when turning right.

Q. **What does this sign mean?**

Ans. * (a) No right turn.
      (b) Turn right.
      (c) Dangerous bend to the right ahead.

Q. **What does this sign mean?**

Ans.   (a)   Cul-de-sac to the left.

        (b)   Roundabout ahead with no left exit.

   *   (c)   No left turn.

Q. **What does this sign mean?**

Ans.   (a)   Slippery road ahead.

   *   (b)   'U'-turn not permitted.

        (c)   Reversing not permitted.

Q. **What does this sign mean?**

Ans.   (a)   Minimum speed is 30 m.p.h.

        (b)   Motorway continues for 30 miles.

   *   (c)   Maximum speed is 30 m.p.h.

Q. **What does this sign mean?**

Ans. *   (a)   Maximum speed is 50 m.p.h.

        (b)   Distance to junction is 50 metres.

        (c)   Maximum permitted weight is 50 tonnes.

Q. **What does this sign mean?**

Ans. (a) 70 metres to end of motorway.
      (b) Minimum speed 70 m.p.h.
    * (c) Maximum speed 70 m.p.h.

Q. **What does this sign mean?**

Ans. * (a) General speed limit applies.
      (b) No entry.
      (c) No parking zone.

Q. **What do these signs together mean?**

Ans. * (a) Parking permitted at times shown.
      (b) Parking prohibited.
      (c) Parking reserved for people with disabilities.

Luan - Aoine
0700 - 0930
MON. - FRI.

Q. **What does this sign mean?**

Ans. (a) Parking permitted.
    * (b) Parking prohibited.
      (c) Private vehicles prohibited.

Q. **What do these signs together mean?**

Ans.

    (a)   Crossroads ahead with roads of equal importance.

    (b)   Pedestrianised street - no access for vehicles.

* (c)   Clearway - no stopping or parking during the times shown.

Q. **What does this sign mean?**

Ans.

* (a)   Disc parking operates during the times shown.

    (b)   Parking allowed during the hours shown.

    (c)   Parking prohibited during the hours shown.

Q. **What does this sign mean?**

Ans.

    (a)   You may park when the rank is empty.

    (b)   You may pick up or set down passengers.

* (c)   Appointed stand for taxis

Q. **What do these signs together mean?**

Ans.   (a)   Bicycle race track.
   *   (b)   Start of cycle track.
       (c)   Track reserved for motorcyclists.

Q. **What does this sign mean?**

Ans.   (a)   Area reserved for children learning to ride bicycles.
       (b)   Cyclists must dismount and walk.
   *   (c)   Shared cycle/pedestrian track.

Q. **What does this sign mean?**

Ans.   (a)   No access. Pedestrianised street ahead.
   *   (b)   Stop.
       (c)   Pedestrian crossing ahead.

Q. **What do these signs together mean?**

Ans.   (a)   Parking not allowed.

(b)   Access for buses and taxis only.

*   (c)   Pedestrianised street ahead - traffic not allowed during the hours indicated.

Luan - Aoine
0700 - 0930
MON. - FRI.

Q. **What does this sign mean?**

Ans. * (a)   Maximum permitted weight is 3 tonnes.

(b)   3 axled vehicles not permitted.

(c)   Vehicles not permitted after 3 a.m.

Q. **What does this sign mean?**

Ans.   (a)   Vehicles weighing more than 10 tonnes per axle not permitted.

*   (b)   Vehicle weight restriction of 10 tonnes.

(c)   Vehicles exceeding 10 metres in length not permitted.

Q.   **What does this sign mean?**

Ans.   (a)   Racing track ahead.

    (b)   Car transporter unloading area.

    * (c)   Axle weight restriction of 4 tonnes.

Q.   **What does this sign mean?**

Ans.   (a)   Maximum permitted weight of vehicle is figure indicated.

    (b)   Maximum permitted length of vehicle is figure indicated.

    * (c)   Maximum permitted height of vehicle is figure indicated.

Q.   **What does this sign mean?**

Ans.   * (a)   Parking of vehicles exceeding the weight shown is not allowed.

    (b)   Passing other traffic which exceed the weight shown is prohibited.

    (c)   Parking in loading area is not allowed.

Q. **What does this sign mean?**

Ans. (a) Speed limit must be observed.
* (b) No overtaking.
(c) Double parking not allowed.

Q. **What do these signs together mean?**

Ans. (a) Outside the hours indicated, only buses, cyclists and taxis are allowed to use the lane.
* (b) Only buses, cyclists and taxis are allowed to use the lane during the hours indicated.
(c) Bus drivers should be aware of cyclists when stopping at bus stops.

Luan - Aoine
0700 - 0930
MON. - FRI.

Q. **What does this sign mean?**

Ans. (a) Cyclists may overtake on the left.
(b) Bus stop reserved for passengers and cyclists.
* (c) 'With-flow' bus lane ahead nearside.

Q.   What does this sign mean?

Ans.   *   (a)   'With-flow' bus lane.
           (b)   Parking for buses and cyclists only.
           (c)   Cycle-track may be crossed by buses.

Q.   What does this sign mean?

Ans.   *   (a)   Bus lane ahead offside.
           (b)   Cyclists must give way to buses ahead.
           (c)   Buses must give way to cyclists ahead.

Q.   What does this sign mean?

Ans.   (a)   Buses may block cyclists from your view.
           (b)   Bus and cycle park ahead.
       *   (c)   With-flow bus lane offside .

Q.   What does this sign mean?

Ans.   (a)   Main bus station ahead.
           (b)   Two-way traffic system ahead.
       *   (c)   Contra-flow bus lane ahead.

Q. **What does this sign mean?**

Ans. * (a) Buses will approach from the right.

(b) Buses will proceed to the right.

(c) Passengers will queue to the right.

Q. **What does this sign mean?**

Ans. * (a) Buses will approach from the left.

(b) Buses will proceed to the left.

(c) Passengers will queue to the left.

WARNING SIGNS

Q. **What does this sign mean?**

Ans. * (a) Junction ahead with roads of lesser importance.
(b) Junction ahead with roads of greater importance.
(c) Junction ahead with roads of equal importance.

Q. **What does this sign mean?**

Ans. (a) Stop at the junction ahead.
* (b) Main road bears to the left.
(c) Main road bears to the right.

Q. **What does this sign mean?**

Ans. (a) Traffic-calming ramps ahead.
(b) Cul-de-sacs to both left and right.
* (c) Staggered crossroads ahead.

Q. **What does this sign mean?**

Ans. (a) Clearway - no stopping or parking during the times shown.
* (b) Crossroads ahead with roads of equal importance.
(c) Pedestrianised street - no vehicles allowed.

Q. **What does this sign mean?**

Ans. (a) No entry.
(b) You have right of way over all other traffic.
* (c) Junction ahead with roads of equal importance.

Q. **What does this sign mean?**

Ans. (a) Major road ahead.
(b) Railway crossing ahead.
* (c) Junction ahead with roads of equal importance.

Q. **What does this sign mean?**

Ans. * (a) Junction ahead with roads of equal importance.
(b) You must stop and yield to traffic ahead.
(c) Traffic island ahead - pass either side.

Q. **What does this sign mean?**

Ans. * (a) Major road ahead.
(b) T-junction ahead with road of greater importance.
(c) The road you are on goes under a bridge.

Q. **What does this sign mean?**

Ans. (a) Cul-de-sac to the right.
* (b) Junction ahead with a road of major importance.
(c) Junction ahead with a road of minor importance.

Q. **What does this sign mean?**

Ans. (a) Level crossing ahead guarded by gates.
* (b) Dual-carriageway ahead.
(c) Two-way traffic ahead.

Q. **What does this sign mean?**

Ans. (a) Low bridge ahead.
(b) Speed ramps ahead.
* (c) 'T'-junction with dual-carriageway ahead.

Q. **What does this sign mean?**

Ans. * (a) Traffic merging from the left.
(b) Traffic from the left has priority.
(c) End of dual-carriageway.

Q.   **What does this sign mean?**

Ans.   (a)   Road narrows briefly.
     *   (b)   Traffic merging/diverging ahead.
             (c)   Clearway at junction ahead.

Q.   **What does this sign mean?**

Ans.   (a)   One-way street ahead.
             (b)   All traffic must turn left.
     *   (c)   Roundabout ahead.

Q.   **What does this sign mean?**

Ans. * (a)   Mini-roundabout ahead.
             (b)   'U'-turn permitted ahead.
             (c)   Roadworks ahead - diversion in operation.

Q.   **What does this sign mean?**

Ans.   (a)   One-way street ahead.
             (b)   Roadworks ahead.
     *   (c)   Dangerous corner ahead.

Q.   **What does this sign mean?**

Ans.   (a)   No left turn.
             (b)   Turn left.
     *   (c)   Dangerous bend ahead.

Q. **What does this sign mean?**

Ans. (a) Descent ahead with speed reduction lanes.
  (b) Temporary surface ahead. Keep left.
* (c) Series of dangerous corners ahead.

Q. **What does this sign mean?**

Ans. (a) Slippery road ahead.
  (b) Diversion ahead.
* (c) Series of dangerous bends ahead.

Q. **What does this sign mean?**

Ans. (a) Traffic from the left has priority.
* (b) Sharp change of direction ahead.
  (c) Road closed. You must turn back.

Q. **What does this sign mean?**

Ans. (a) Overtake on the right only.
  (b) Left hand lane has an uneven surface.
* (c) Road narrows on one side.

Q   **What does this sign mean?**

Ans.   (a)   Dual-carriageway ahead.

          (b)   Railway crossing ahead.

      * (c)   Road narrows ahead.

Q.   **What does this sign mean?**

Ans. * (a)   Road divides up ahead.

          (b)   Heavy vehicles have priority.

          (c)   Lay-by ahead.

Q.   **What does this sign mean?**

Ans.   (a)   Tunnel ahead.

          (b)   Oncoming traffic has
                   priority.

      * (c)   Dual-carriageway ends.

Q.   **What does this sign mean?**

Ans.   (a)   One-way street.

          (b)   Dual-carriageway ahead.

      * (c)   Two-way traffic ahead.

Q.   **What does this sign mean?**

Ans.   (a)   River or unprotected quay
                   ahead.

      * (b)   Steep descent ahead.

          (c)   Sharp climb ahead.

Q.   **What does this sign mean?**

Ans.   *   (a)   Steep ascent ahead.
             (b)   Hump-backed bridge ahead.
             (c)   Caravan and picnic area
                   ahead.

Q.   **What does this sign mean?**

Ans.   (a)   Maximum permitted weight
                     up ahead is figure indicated.
         *   (b)   Restricted headroom up
                     ahead.
             (c)   Restricted road width up
                   ahead.

Q.   **What does this sign mean?**

Ans.   *   (a)   Overhead electric cables.
             (b)   Underground electric cables.
             (c)   Radio transmission mast
                   ahead.

Q.   **What does this sign mean?**

Ans.   (a)   Major road works ahead.
         *   (b)   Level crossing ahead
                     unguarded by gates or
                     barriers.
             (c)   Machinery crossing ahead.

Q. **What does this sign mean?**

Ans. * (a) Level crossing ahead guarded by gates or barriers.
      (b) Farm machinery crossing ahead.
      (c) Private grounds. No entry.

Q. **What does this sign mean?**

Ans. (a) Railway station ahead.
   * (b) Level crossing ahead with lights and barriers.
      (c) Railway bridge ahead.

Q. **What does this sign mean?**

Ans. (a) You must stop when you see brake lights ahead.
      (b) Emerging vehicles have priority. You must stop if necessary.
  * (c) Stop when red lights show.

> STOP
> When
> Red Lights
> Show

> STOP
> *nuair a lasann na*
> *soilse dearga*

Q. **What does this sign mean?**

Ans. * (a) Automatic level crossing ahead.
      (b) Bridge may be raised ahead.
      (c) Traffic lights may be activated by passing traffic.

> SLOW
> Automatic
> Level Crossing

> GO MALL
> *Crosaire*
> *Comhréidh*
> *Uathoibríoch*

Q.　　**What does this sign mean?**

Ans.　　(a)　Road reflective studs ahead.
　　　　(b)　Series of bumps or hollows ahead.
　　*　(c)　Sharp rise in the road ahead e.g. hump-back bridge.

Q.　　**What does this sign mean?**

Ans.　　(a)　Low bridge ahead.
　　*　(b)　Sharp depression ahead.
　　　　(c)　Road divides up ahead. Pass left or right.

Q.　　**What does this sign mean?**

Ans.　　(a)　Steep hills.
　　*　(b)　Series of bumps or hollows ahead.
　　　　(c)　Industrial estate ahead.

Q.　　**What does this sign mean?**

Ans.　　(a)　Series of bends ahead.
　　*　(b)　Slippery stretch of road ahead.
　　　　(c)　Steep hill ahead.

Q.   **What does this sign mean?**

Ans.   *   (a)   Quay, canal, or river ahead without barrier.
            (b)   Steep descent ahead.
            (c)   Slippery road ahead.

Q.   **What does this sign mean?**

Ans.   (a)   Train crossing ahead.
     *   (b)   Traffic signals ahead.
            (c)   School children crossing ahead.

Q.   **What does this sign mean?**

Ans.   *   (a)   School ahead.
            (b)   Children's play area ahead.
            (c)   Zebra crossing ahead.

Q.   **What does this sign mean?**

Ans.   (a)   Picnic and play area ahead.
            (b)   Level crossing ahead with pedestrian walkway.
     *   (c)   School children crossing ahead.

Q. **What does this sign mean?**

Ans.   (a)   School playground ahead.
        (b)   Children's play area ahead.
     * (c)   School children crossing ahead.

Q. **What do these signs together mean?**

Ans. * (a)   Children crossing.
        (b)   People jogging have right of way.
        (c)   Loose chippings ahead on the road.

Q. **What does this sign mean?**

Ans. * (a)   Possibility of riders on horseback ahead.
        (b)   Entrance to horse riding school.
        (c)   No riding on horseback ahead.

Q. **What does this sign mean?**

Ans. * (a)   Possibility of cattle or farm animals ahead.
        (b)   Livestock mart ahead.
        (c)   Veterinary station ahead.

Q. **What does this sign mean?**

Ans.
     (a)   Abbatoir ahead.
* (b)   Possibility of sheep ahead.
     (c)   Woollen mills ahead.

Q. **What does this sign mean?**

Ans.
     (a)   Stag-hunting up ahead.
     (b)   Wildlife reserve - no stopping.
* (c)   Possibility of deer or wild animals up ahead.

Q. **What does this sign mean?**

Ans.
     (a)   Airport ahead.
* (b)   Crosswinds.
     (c)   Nature reserve. Do not throw litter.

Q. **What does this sign mean?**

Ans. * (a)   Pedestrian crossing ahead.
       (b)   Lane reserved for pedestrians.
       (c)   Beware of pedestrians at night.

Q.   **What does this sign mean?**

Ans.   (a)   Cathedral or church up
                   ahead.
             (b)   Historic site up ahead.
      *   (c)   Tunnel ahead.

Q.   **What does this sign mean?**

Ans. * (a)   Danger of falling rocks up
                   ahead.
             (b)   Rugged coast up ahead.
             (c)   Danger of oil spill up ahead.

Q   **What does this sign mean?**

Ans.   (a)   Airport ahead.
      *   (b)   Possibility of low flying
                   aircraft.
             (c)   Direction of prevailing wind.

Q.   **What does this sign mean?**

Ans.   (a)   You may not overtake.
             (b)   You may not park.
      *   (c)   Drive on the left-hand side.

MOTORWAY SIGNS

Q. **What does this sign mean?**

Ans.   (a)   No learner drivers.
   * (b)   Motorway ahead.
      (c)   No slow vehicles.

Q. **What does this sign mean?**

Ans.   (a)   Toll-bridge ahead.
   * (b)   Entry to motorway.
      (c)   High-sided vehicles should beware of cross winds.

Q. **What does this sign mean?**

Ans.   (a)   No overtaking for 500 metres.
   * (b)   Motorway ends 500 metres ahead.
      (c)   Low bridge 500 metres ahead.

Q. **What does this sign mean?**

Ans.   (a)   Crossing onto the opposite carriageway is not allowed.
      (b)   No overtaking.
   * (c)   End of motorway.

Q. **What does this sign mean?**

Ans. (a) Three lanes ahead.
   (b) Crossing traffic ahead.
 * (c) Three hundred metres to
   the next exit.

Q. **What does this sign mean?**

Ans. (a) Dual-carriageway crossing
   ahead.
 * (b) Two hundred metres to the
   next exit.
   (c) You must stay in your lane.

Q. **What does this sign mean?**

Ans. * (a) One hundred metres to the
   next exit.
   (b) Single carriageway ahead.
   (c) Low bridge ahead.

ROAD SIGNS

Q. **What does this sign mean?**

Ans. (a) Heavy snowfall ahead.
 * (b) Roadworks ahead.
   (c) Building site ahead.

Q. **What does this sign mean?**

Ans. (a) Steep hill ahead.
  * (b) Uneven surface ahead.
   (c) Industrial estate ahead.

Q. **What does this sign mean?**

Ans. (a) Series of bends ahead.
  * (b) Slippery stretch of road ahead.
   (c) Steep hill ahead.

Q. **What does this sign mean?**

Ans. (a) Overtake on the right only.
   (b) Left-hand lane has an uneven surface.
  * (c) Road narrows from left-hand side.

Q. **What does this sign mean?**

Ans. (a) Overtake on the right only.
   (b) Left-hand lane has an uneven surface.
  * (c) Road narrows from right-hand side.

Q. **What does this sign mean?**

Ans. (a) Dual-carriageway ahead.
     (b) Railway crossing ahead.
  * (c) Road narrows ahead.

Q. **What does this sign mean?**

Ans. (a) Football stadium ahead.
     (b) Litter is not allowed.
  * (c) Manual traffic control ahead.

Q. **What does this sign mean?**

Ans. (a) Train crossing ahead.
  * (b) Traffic lights ahead.
     (c) School children crossing
            ahead.

Q. **What does this sign mean?**

Ans. (a) One-way street.
     (b) Dual-carriageway ahead.
  * (c) Two-way traffic.

Q. **What does this sign mean?**

Ans. (a) You must not overtake.
  * (b) Left-hand lane closed ahead.
     (c) Stop sign ahead.

Q.   **What does this sign mean?**

Ans.   (a)   No left turn ahead.

              (b)   Do not drive on the hard
                     shoulder.

        *   (c)   Left-hand lane closed ahead.

Q.   **What does this sign mean?**

Ans.   (a)   Dual-carriageway ahead.

        *   (b)   Middle lane closed ahead.

              (c)   'T'-junction ahead.

Q.   **What does this sign mean?**

Ans.   (a)   Series of dangerous corners
                     ahead.

        *   (b)   Right-hand lane closed
                     ahead.

              (c)   Entry to dual carriageway
                     ahead.

Q.   **What does this sign mean?**

Ans.   (a)   Faster traffic should use the
                     right-hand lanes.

              (b)   Overtake only on the right.

        *   (c)   Left-hand lane closed ahead.

Q. **What does this sign mean?**

Ans. (a) Dual-carriageway slip lane ahead.

* (b) Middle lane closed ahead.

(c) Make way for oncoming traffic.

Q. **What does this sign mean?**

Ans. (a) 'T'-junction ahead.

(b) Major road ahead.

* (c) No through road.

Q. **What does this sign mean?**

Ans. * (a) Pedestrians keep right.

(b) Do not drive on the footpath.

(c) Shopping mall on the right.

Q. **At road works, when a flagman displays this sign, you should .....**

Ans. (a) make a detour.

(b) stop.

* (c) proceed with caution.

Q. At road works, when a flagman displays this sign, you should .....

Ans.
    (a)   make a detour.
* (b)   stop.
    (c)   go.

Q. What do these signs together mean?

Ans.
    (a)   End of road.
    (b)   End of speed limit.
* (c)   End of detour.

Q. What does this sign mean?

Ans. *
    (a)   Crossover to left-hand side.
    (b)   Slow lane ahead for heavy traffic.
    (c)   Lay-by ahead.

Q. What does this sign mean?

Ans.
    (a)   End of "no overtaking" zone.
    (b)   Traffic calming measures ahead.
* (c)   Traffic crossover ahead due to roadworks.

Q. **What does this sign mean?**

Ans. * (a) Traffic flow divides at road works.
       (b) Heavy vehicles have priority.
       (c) Lay-by ahead.

Q. **What does this sign mean?**

Ans. * (a) End of traffic separation at roadworks.
       (b) Lighter vehicles should use the middle lane.
       (c) Beware of vehicles with a wide load.

HAND SIGNALS

Q. **What does this hand signal mean?**

Ans. (a) The cyclist intends to slow down or stop.
      (b) The cyclist intends to turn left.
    * (c) The cyclist intends to move out or to turn right.

Q. **What does this hand signal mean?**

Ans. (a) The cyclist intends to move out or to turn right.

* (b) The cyclist intends to slow down or stop.

(c) The cyclist is signalling following traffic to overtake.

Q. **What does this hand signal mean?**

Ans. * (a) The cyclist intends to go straight on.

(b) The cyclist is waving to say 'hello'.

(c) The cyclist is yielding right of way to you.

Q. **What does this hand signal mean?**

Ans. * (a) The cyclist intends to turn left.

(b) The cyclist intends to overtake.

(c) The cyclist intends to dismount.

Q. **What does this hand signal mean?**

Ans. * (a) The cyclist intends to turn right.
(b) The cyclist intends to slow down.
(c) The cyclist intends to stop for pedestrians.

Q. **What does this hand signal mean?**

Ans. (a) The cyclist intends to stop.
(b) The cyclist intends to cross the road.
* (c) The cyclist intends to turn left.

Q. **What does this hand signal mean?**

Ans. * (a) The driver intends to turn left.
(b) The driver intends to turn right.
(c) The driver intends to slow down or stop.

Q. **What does this hand signal mean?**

Ans. (a) The driver intends to turn left.

(b) The driver intends to do a 'U'-turn.

* (c) The driver intends to move out or turn right.

Q. **What does this hand signal mean?**

Ans. (a) The driver intends to turn left.

* (b) The driver intends to slow down or stop.

(c) The driver intends to turn right.

Q. **What does this hand signal mean?**

Ans. (a) The driver is cleaning the window.

(b) The driver is telling you to turn right.

* (c) The driver intends to turn left.

Q. **What does this hand signal mean?**

Ans.   (a)   The driver is telling other drivers to slow down.

*   (b)   The driver intends to turn right.

  (c)   The driver intends to slow down or stop.

Q. **What does this hand signal mean?**

Ans. * (a)   The driver intends to go straight ahead.

  (b)   The driver intends to reverse.

  (c)   The driver is signalling you to proceed.

GARDA SIGNALS

Q. **What does this Garda signal mean?**

Ans. * (a)   Halt if approaching from the front.

  (b)   Proceed if approaching from the front.

  (c)   Halt if approaching from behind.

Q. **What does this Garda signal mean?**

Ans.   (a)   Turn left.
     *   (b)   Halt if approaching from behind.
        (c)   Halt if approaching from the front.

Q. **What does this Garda signal mean?**

Ans. *   (a)   Halt if approaching from either front or rear.
        (b)   Halt if approaching from the front.
        (c)   Halt if approaching from the rear.

Q. **What does this Garda signal mean?**

Ans.   (a)   You must not proceed to the left.
        (b)   To beckon on traffic approaching from the front.
     *   (c)   To beckon on traffic approaching from either side.

Q.   **What does this Garda signal mean?**

Ans. * (a) To beckon on traffic approaching from the front.

        (b) To beckon on traffic approaching from the left.

        (c) To beckon on traffic approaching from the right.

ROAD MARKINGS

Q.   **What does this road marking mean?**

Ans.   (a) Cycle lane ahead.

        (b) Traffic-calming ahead.

  * (c) Stop and give way to pedestrians.

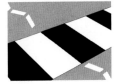

Q.   **What does this road marking mean?**

Ans.   (a) Speed control ramp ahead.

  * (b) Stop and give way to pedestrians.

        (c) You are entering a built-up area.

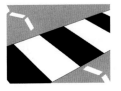

Q. **What does this road marking mean?**

Ans. * (a) Pedestrian crossing nearby.
(b) Maximum speed limit is 20 m.p.h.
(c) You may park for a maximum of 1 hour only.

Q. **What does this road marking mean?**

Ans. * (a) Do not enter unless your exit is clear or unless you are turning right.
(b) Traffic from right and left have right-of-way.
(c) You have right-of-way over traffic from both right and left.

Q. **What does this road marking mean?**

Ans. (a) You may overtake.
(b) You are approaching a stop sign.
* (c) You must not cross the line.

Q.   **White arrows painted on the road.....**

Ans. * (a)   indicate which lane you should use for the direction which you intend to take.
            (b)   mean that heavy vehicles should separate from lighter traffic.
            (c)   mean that the lane is reserved for buses only.

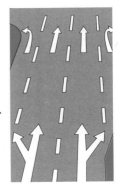

Q.   **What does this road marking and sign together mean?**

Ans.   (a)   No parking at any time.
            (b)   Parking allowed during business hours.
        * (c)   Parking not allowed at the times shown.

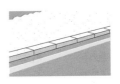

Q.   **What does this road marking and information plate together mean?**

Ans.   (a)   Taxi rank.
        * (b)   Parking not allowed at the times shown.
            (c)   No parking at any time.

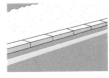

Q. **What does this road marking mean?**

Ans.   (a)   You may overtake provided you do not cross the broken white line.

         (b)   You may not overtake.

*   (c)   You may not cross the broken white line unless it is safe to do so.

Q. **If driving from right to left, what does this road marking mean?**

Ans.   (a)   Speed restrictions apply on both carriageways.

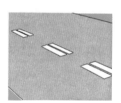

*   (b)   A continuous white line lies ahead.

         (c)   All traffic must keep to the left of the broken white lines.

Q. If driving from right to left, may you cross the continuous white line?

Ans. (a) Yes, provided there is no oncoming traffic.

* (b) No.

(c) Yes

Q. If driving from left to right, may you cross from the broken white line side to the other side?

Ans. (a) Yes, only when turning right.

* (b) Yes, provided it is safe to do so.

(c) No.

Q. What does this road marking mean?

Ans. (a) Pedestrian crossing.

(b) The road ahead is a cul-de-sac.

* (c) No entry.

Q. **What does this road marking mean?**

Ans.   (a)   Keep outside the yellow lines.

    *   (b)   Parking prohibited at all times.

      (c)   Parking prohibited during business hours.

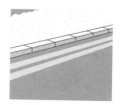

Q.   **What does this road marking mean?**

Ans.   *   (a)   You must keep left of the continuous white line.

      (b)   You may overtake provided there is no oncoming traffic.

      (c)   Traffic on either side of the continuous white line can overtake provided it is safe to do so.

Q. **What does the broken yellow line road marking mean?**

Ans. (a) No stopping for any reason except in an emergency.

(b) Slow lane for heavy vehicles only.

* (c) The edge of the carriageway/hard shoulder.

TRAFFIC LIGHTS

Q. **What does this traffic light mean?**

Ans * (a) Do not proceed unless it is safe to do so.

(b) Railway crossing ahead.

(c) Major road works ahead.

Q. **What does this traffic light mean?**

Ans. (a) You may proceed if the way is clear.

* (b) Only proceed if you cannot stop safely.

(c) Stop.

Q. **What does this traffic light mean?**

Ans. (a) Stop and wait until the full green light appears.

(b) All traffic must turn right.

* (c) You may proceed in the direction of the green arrow.

Q. **What does this traffic light mean?**

Ans. (a) All traffic must turn left only.

* (b) Left turning traffic may proceed.

(c) Traffic is not allowed to turn left.

Q. **What does this traffic light mean?**

Ans. * (a) You must stop.

(b) You may proceed.

(c) Stop if you can do so safely.

Q. **What does this traffic light mean?**

Ans.   (a)   You must stop.
   *   (b)   You may proceed if the way is clear.
   (c)   You must give way to oncoming traffic.

Q. **What colour traffic light comes after the green?**

Ans.   (a)   Red.
   *   (b)   Amber.
   (c)   Red or amber.

Q. **When traffic lights are green you should not proceed when .....**

Ans.   *   (a)   by doing so, your vehicle would block the junction.
   (b)   buses are stopped waiting to turn from the road on your right.
   (c)   buses are stopped waiting to turn from the road on your left.

Q. What colour traffic light comes on after a flashing amber light?

Ans.   (a)   Red.
    * (b)   Green.
      (c)   Red or green.

Q. What traffic light comes on after a non-flashing amber light?

Ans * (a)   Red.
      (b)   Green.
      (c)   Red or Green.

Q. What do flashing amber lights at a Pelican Crossing mean?

Ans.   (a)   Danger ahead - you must stop and wait until they stop flashing.
      (b)   You are entering a special speed limit area.
  * (c)   Stop and give way to pedestrians, but proceed if the way is clear.

SPEED LIMITS

Q. What is the General Speed Limit?

Ans. * (a)   60 m.p.h.
      (b)   70 m.p.h.
      (c)   80 m.p.h.

Q. The maximum permissable speed for cars on motorways is .....

Ans.
    (a)   60 m.p.h.
* (b)   70 m.p.h.
    (c)   80 m.p.h.

Q. The maximum permissable speed for motorcycles on motorways is .....

Ans.
    (a)   60 m.p.h.
* (b)   70 m.p.h.
    (c)   80 m.p.h.

Q. What is the maximum permitted speed of a car towing a caravan?

Ans.
    (a)   30 m.p.h.
    (b)   40 m.p.h.
* (c)   50 m.p.h.

Q. What is the maximum permitted speed of a car towing a trailer:

Ans.
    (a)   40 m.p.h.
* (b)   50 m.p.h.
    (c)   55 m.p.h.

OTHER REGULATORY MATTERS

Q. The maximum permitted blood-alcohol level for driving is .....

Ans.
    (a)   100 mg per 100 ml.
    (b)   50 mg per 100 ml.
* (c)   80 mg per 100 ml.

Q. You have been stopped at a Garda checkpoint and asked to blow into a breathalyser. What should you do?

Ans. * (a)   Blow into the breathalyser.
    (b)   Demand to see your solicitor.
    (c)   Refuse to use the breathalyser but offer to give a blood or urine sample.

Q. 'Lighting up hours' are .....

Ans. * (a)   from half an hour after sunset to half an hour before sunrise.
    (b)   from mid-night until 6 a.m.
    (c)   when visibility is less than 200 metres.

Q. What lights should your vehicle show at dusk?

Ans. * (a)   Side lamps or dipped headlights.
    (b)   Full headlamps.
    (c)   No lights.

Q. **You may not park .....**

Ans. * (a) at or near a bend.
  (b) where there is a broken white line along the centre of the road.
  (c) in a lit-up area.

Q. **When approaching a zebra crossing, you may not park within what distance of the crossing?**

Ans. * (a) 15 metres.
  (b) 10 metres.
  (c) 5 metres.

Q. **You may not park your vehicle within what distance of a junction?**

Ans. (a) 15 metres.
  * (b) 5 metres.
  (c) 3 metres.

Q. **You wish to park your vehicle and the only available space is at a bus stop. You may .....**

Ans. (a) park for a maximum of 10 minutes.
  (b) park for a maximum of 30 minutes.
  * (c) never park at a bus stop.

Q. **When may you park your vehicle at an entrance to a property?**

Ans.   (a)   For a few minutes when you are in a hurry.

*   (b)   Never, except with the property owner's consent.

(c)   For a maximum of 10 minutes at any one time.

Q. **When may you park your vehicle on a footpath?**

Ans   *   (a)   Never.

(b)   For a maximum of 15 minutes.

(c)   When no other space is available.

Q. **When may you double-park your vehicle?**

Ans.   (a)   Where the road is wide.

(b)   When you are opposite an entrance.

*   (c)   Never.

Q. **When may you park your vehicle at a taxi rank?**

Ans.   *   (a)   Never.

(b)   When parking for less than 30 minutes.

(c)   When the rank is unoccupied.

Q. **When may you park your vehicle at a sharp bend?**

Ans.   (a)   When drivers coming from behind can see your vehicle.
*   (b)   Never.
       (c)   When you put on your hazard warning lights.

Q. **When may you park your vehicle on the brow of a hill?**

Ans.   (a)   When it has an efficient handbrake.
       (b)   When you angle the wheels towards the kerb.
*   (c)   Never.

Q. **When may you overtake another vehicle on the left-hand side?**

Ans.   (a)   Never
       (b)   When there is sufficient space to do so.
*   (c)   When the vehicle in front is signalling to turn right, or in slow-moving lanes of traffic.

Q. **The on-the-spot fine for exceeding the speed limit is .....**

Ans.   (a)   £20.
*   (b)   £50.
       (c)   £100.

Q. What is the purpose of 'rumble' strips?

Ans. * (a) To warn drivers to reduce speed if necessary.
(b) To warn drivers that there is a stop sign ahead.
(c) To warn drivers that they are entering a speed limit area.

Q. When may a trailer be towed on a public road without a rear number plate?

Ans. (a) When the tailboard is removed.
* (b) Never.
(c) When carrying a load which overhangs the rear of the trailer.

ALERT DRIVING, AND CONSIDERATION FOR ROAD USERS

ANTICIPATION

Q. When there is a sharp dip in the road ahead, you should .....

Ans. * (a) reduce your speed, keep to the left and be alert for a parked vehicle which may be hidden from your view.

(b) increase your speed.

(c) move to the centre of the road in order to avoid a vehicle which may be parked in the dip on your side of the road.

Q. When you see a red warning triangle on the road up ahead, you should .....

Ans. (a) avoid it, maintain speed and carry on.

(b) stop before you get to it.

* (c) slow down and watch for a hazard up ahead.

Q. When you are approaching traffic lights which you know to have been 'green' for some time, you should .....

Ans. (a) maintain your speed.

(b) accelerate in order to clear them before they change.

* (c) prepare to stop in case they may change before you reach them.

Q. You are approaching a junction which is controlled by traffic lights. They are temporarily out of order. You should .....

Ans.
   (a) drive smartly through the junction in order to avoid delay.

   (b) switch on your hazard warning lights and drive on.

* (c) drive cautiously while watching out for other traffic.

Q. When you are driving along and see cattle on the road up ahead, you should .....

Ans.
   (a) sound the horn to try to get the cattle to move aside.

   (b) switch on your headlights and try to pass as quickly as possible.

* (c) reduce speed and overtake with care.

Q. As you approach a hump-backed hill, you should .....

Ans. * (a) reduce speed, keep to the left and be alert for any parked vehicle which may be hidden from your view.

   (b) press the clutch pedal and sound the horn as a warning.

   (c) maintain normal speed and road position.

CONSIDERATION

Q.   There are pedestrians on the footpath up
            ahead and there are pools of water on the
            road. You should .....

Ans.   (a)   brake suddenly as you approach the pools of
                    water.
            (b)   sound the horn as a warning to the
                    pedestrians and continue on.
        *   (c)   reduce speed and try to avoid the pools of
                    water so as not to splash the pedestrians.

Q.   You are about to stop and notice that the
            vehicle behind you is towing a trailer.
            You should .....

Ans.   (a)   stop quickly keeping a close eye on the rear-
                    view mirror.
            (b)   use the hand brake to stop.
        *   (c)   indicate in good time, pull up gradually,
                    allowing the vehicle behind you extra
                    stopping distance.

Q.   A bus up ahead is beginning to pull out from
            a bus stop. You should .....

Ans.   (a)   try to get past it to avoid being delayed.
        *   (b)   slow down and allow it to move out.
            (c)   drive alongside it because you have right-of-
                    way.

Q. What should you do on a narrow road when another vehicle is coming in the opposite direction?

Ans.
    (a)   Maintain your position and expect the other vehicle to move over if necessary.

   * (b)   Reduce speed and ensure that you allow reasonable clearance between your vehicle and the oncoming one, before proceeding.

    (c)   Drive along the middle of the road to encourage the other driver to pull in.

Q. You are driving along and wish to call into a shop on the side of the street in order to make a purchase. You should .....

Ans.
    (a)   park on the footpath so as not to impede the free flow of traffic on the road.

    (b)   switch on your hazard warning lights and park slightly up on the footpath.

   * (c)   continue on until you find a proper parking space.

Q. When driving behind another vehicle which you do not intend to overtake, you should .....

Ans.
    (a)   drive close behind it in order to let following traffic overtake both vehicles.

    (b)   signal to following traffic to overtake both vehicles.

   * (c)   keep well back to allow following traffic to overtake you.

Q. You are driving in a line of traffic and do not intend to overtake. You should .....

Ans.
    (a)   drive close to the vehicle in front.
    (b)   maintain your speed.
* (c)   stay back and leave a gap for other drivers who may wish to overtake you.

Q. If you do not stay well back from a vehicle which you do not intend to overtake .....

Ans. * (a)   other drivers may attempt to overtake both vehicles reducing the clearance for oncoming drivers.
    (b)   air turbulence from the vehicle in front could blow your vehicle off course.
    (c)   there will always be sufficient clearance for following drivers to overtake you and the vehicle in front.

Q. If you do not stay well back behind another vehicle which you do not intend to overtake .....

Ans. * (a)   it may be more difficult for following traffic to overtake you.
    (b)   it would be easier for following traffic to overtake you.
    (c)   following traffic will not always see the vehicle in front of your vehicle.

Q.   If you do not stay well back behind another vehicle which you do not intend to overtake .....

Ans.   (a)   it would be easier for following traffic to overtake you.

*   (b)   following drivers may attempt to overtake both vehicles reducing the clearance for oncoming drivers.

(c)   following traffic will not always see the vehicle in front of your vehicle.

Q.   When driving along behind another vehicle which you do not intend to overtake, you should .....

Ans.   *   (a)   stay well back to allow following traffic to overtake you.

(b)   drive close behind the vehicle in front.

(c)   beckon to following drivers when it is safe for them to overtake you.

Q.   Tailgating (driving too close behind the vehicle in front) is dangerous because .....

Ans.   (a)   you will be exceeding the speed limit.

(b)   your braking system is less efficient.

*   (c)   there is not sufficient space to allow you to stop in an emergency without colliding with the vehicle in front.

Q. When you wish to use a mobile phone while driving, you should .....

Ans. * (a) pull in and stop.
(b) reduce speed and be alert for other road users.
(c) allow a wider gap to open up with the vehicle in front and continue at normal speed.

ALERTNESS

Q. What danger can arise during daylight when you are driving into an area which is heavily shaded by overhanging trees?

Ans. (a) Your vehicle's engine could suddenly run cold.
* (b) Your visibility could be seriously reduced.
(c) Your vehicle's windscreen could fog up.

Q. When you are being overtaken by another vehicle, you should .....

Ans. (a) increase your speed.
(b) move to the right.
* (c) maintain your course and reduce speed if necessary.

Q. You have parked in a row of parked vehicles which other traffic is overtaking. You should ensure that .....

Ans. * (a) you do not open a door without proper care being taken.
(b) there is not a Traffic Warden present.
(c) the gear lever is in the neutral position before getting out.

Q. When and how should signals be given to other road users?

Ans. * (a) Clearly and in good time to warn all other traffic.
(b) When necessary to warn oncoming traffic.
(c) When necessary to warn following traffic.

Q. If you give a late signal, other road users .....

Ans. (a) would not be affected.
* (b) may not have sufficient time in which to react.
(c) would always have sufficient time in which to react.

OBSERVATION / FIELD OF VIEW

VISIBILITY

Q. You wish to overtake the car in front. You should firstly .....

Ans.
(a) indicate and increase your speed.
(b) sound your horn and move out.
* (c) check for oncoming vehicles and check your rear view mirror.

Q. You are at a junction where visibility is extremely limited. You should .....

Ans.
(a) drive the front of your vehicle out onto the other road to enable other drivers to see you.
(b) seek help from a passer-by.
* (c) move out with extreme care, watching carefully to the left and the right.

Q. You should use your vehicle's rear view mirrors when .....

Ans.
(a) reversing only.
* (b) moving off or changing lanes.
(c) changing gears.

Q. How would you proceed if your view was obstructed at a junction?

Ans. * (a) Move out slowly onto the road while watching carefully for other traffic.
   (b) Sound the horn several times and proceed.
   (c) Ask a passer-by to guide you out onto the other road.

Q. In daytime when there are dark clouds, you should .....

Ans. * (a) drive with your side-lights or dipped headlights switched on.
   (b) drive with your full headlights switched on.
   (c) not switch on your lights until 'lighting-up hours'.

Q. When towing a caravan, you should .....

Ans. (a) carry all passengers in the caravan.
   (b) switch on the hazard warning lights.
   * (c) have extended mirrors fitted to your vehicle and use them regularly.

Q. You are driving a vehicle which is towing a high-sided trailer. You should .....

Ans. (a) drive with normal mirrors only.
   (b) drive with full headlights on.
   * (c) make use of extended mirrors where necessary, to check for following traffic.

Q. It is important to have clean, clear, windows .....

Ans. (a) to enable other road users to see you.

(b) to improve the appearance of the vehicle.

* (c) to ensure good all-round visibility from your vehicle.

Q. You wish to undertake a journey and your vehicle windows are covered with ice. You should .....

Ans. (a) clear enough space in the windscreen to be able to see ahead.

(b) drive slowly until the heater and demister have cleared the ice from the windows.

* (c) remove all the ice from the windows before starting.

Q. What action would you take if the vehicle's windows are covered in ice?

Ans. (a) Drive at a reduced speed until the heating system has cleared the ice.

* (b) Switch on the heating system and use a scraper to clear the ice before driving.

(c) Switch on the windscreen wipers.

Q. **What action would you take if condensation was affecting your vehicle's windows?**

Ans. (a) Drive for a few miles with a window open.

(b) Wipe the glass with the back of your hand.

* (c) Dry them initially with a cloth and then use the demister system.

Q. **What effect can sunlight have on grimy windows?**

Ans. (a) It can enhance visibility.

* (b) It can create a mirror effect and reduce visibility.

(c) It can eliminate a heavy build-up of condensation on the windows.

Q. **You are riding a motorcycle in heavy rain. To improve visibility, you should .....**

Ans. (a) increase speed.

* (b) reduce speed.

(c) lift up the visor on your helmet.

Q. **While riding a motorcycle, you could ensure better visibility to other drivers by .....**

Ans. (a) sitting up straight in the saddle.

(b) occasionally weaving slightly from side to side.

* (c) wearing reflective or fluorescent material and a "Sam Browne" belt.

Q. **While riding a motorcycle, you could ensure better visibility to other road users by .....**

Ans. * (a) driving with dipped headlights on.
(b) wearing dark-coloured clothing.
(c) driving crouched over the steering.

BLINDSPOTS

Q. **You are driving behind a heavy goods vehicle which is signalling to make a right-hand turn. You should .....**

Ans. (a) look to see if the vehicle can complete the turn without stopping, and if not, overtake it yourself.
(b) overtake it slowly on the inside by driving partly on the footpath if necessary.
* (c) stay behind until there is sufficient space to overtake it on the inside or until it has completed the turn.

Q. **You are driving behind a bus which is signalling to make a left-hand turn. There is oncoming traffic. You should .....**

Ans. (a) overtake it on the right-hand side.
(b) overtake it on the left-hand side.
* (c) stay back and allow it to complete the turn.

Q.   **What might be described as a bus driver's 'blind' spots?**

Ans.   *   (a)   The areas to the front, sides and rear of the bus which the driver cannot see.

           (b)   The seats at the rear of the bus.

           (c)   The windscreen area covered by the sun-visor.

Q.   **You are driving behind a heavy goods vehicle. What are its 'blind spots'?**

Ans.   *   (a)   The areas to the front, sides and rear which the driver cannot see.

           (b)   Parts of the road ahead which are obscured by other large vehicles.

           (c)   The portion of the windscreen covered by the sun-visor.

Q.   **What are a driver's 'blind spots' when towing a loaded trailer?**

Ans.   *   (a)   The areas to the side and rear which can not be seen through the centre rearview mirror.

           (b)   The view to the front hidden by the sun visor.

           (c)   The number plate and lights on the rear of the trailer.

Q. You are driving on a wide road behind a vehicle which has signalled to turn right up ahead. You should .....

Ans. (a) stay behind until it has completed the turn.
* (b) overtake on the left-hand side and carry on.
(c) overtake on the left but only if you are turning left a short distance ahead.

REVERSING

Q. You wish to reverse your vehicle. You should .....

Ans. (a) turn your steering fully and reverse quickly.
(b) open the door fully to look behind.
* (c) check carefully all around before and during the reverse.

Q. You wish to reverse your vehicle on a busy street. You should .....

Ans. (a) sound the horn occasionally as you reverse.
* (b) reverse slowly, checking all around for other road users.
(c) listen carefully for the sound of other road users.

Q.   When reversing with a trailer, you should .....

Ans.   (a)   sound the horn as a warning.
    (b)   turn the steering in the direction in which you wish to reverse.
*   (c)   look all around and use the rear-view mirrors as you reverse.

OVERTAKING

Q.   When may you overtake another vehicle on the left-hand side?

Ans.   (a)   Never.
    (b)   When there is sufficient space to do so.
*   (c)   When the vehicle in front is signalling to turn right, or in slow-moving lanes of traffic.

U-TURN

Q.   You wish to perform a 'U'-turn.
You should .....

Ans. * (a)   check ahead and behind for approaching traffic.
    (b)   check ahead for approaching traffic.
    (c)   check behind for approaching traffic.

Q.   You wish to turn your vehicle around on the road. You should .....

Ans.   (a)   drive into somebody's driveway and reverse back onto the road.

  *   (b)   check ahead and behind for oncoming traffic and turn briskly while still keeping a look-out.

       (c)   drive onto a footpath, if necessary, in order to ensure that you have sufficient room to turn.

GOOD JUDGMENT AND PERCEPTION

FATIGUE

Q. If you become drowsy while driving, you should .....

Ans.
    (a) turn up the heating.
*   (b) stop, take a break, including a short walk if possible.
    (c) stretch your arms and close your eyes for short periods.

Q. To keep alert during a long journey, you should .....

Ans. * (a) increase the air circulation and make regular stops if necessary.
    (b) increase your speed to shorten the journey.
    (c) keep the radio turned on.

Q. If you are driving and you feel tired, you should .....

Ans.
    (a) increase your speed to shorten the journey time.
    (b) drive along the centre of the road.
*   (c) open a window and/or stop and take a break.

Q. When driving at night how could a warm vehicle interior affect you?

Ans. * (a) It could make you feel drowsy.
(b) It could reassure you that the engine is operating at normal temperatures.
(c) It could increase your sense of alertness.

Q. Exhaust gases leaking into the driver compartment of your vehicle, could cause you .....

Ans. (a) to become more alert.
* (b) to become drowsy or ill.
(c) to be enticed to drive faster than normal.

AWARENESS

Q. If you are behind schedule in arriving at a destination at an appointed time, you should .....

Ans. (a) exceed the speed limit, if necessary, to make up the time.
(b) drive aggressively.
* (c) be patient and drive so as to arrive safely.

Q. When you are driving along in traffic and you do not wish to travel at the same speed as the vehicles in front, you should .....

Ans.
    (a)   keep your position and allow following vehicles to overtake you if they wish.
    (b)   indicate left and keep to the left.
* (c)   keep to the left and allow following vehicles to overtake you if they wish.

Q. You see a school bus stopped on your side of the road up ahead. Which of the following is the most correct action for you to take?

Ans.
    (a)   Sound the horn as a warning and continue on.
    (b)   Carry on regardless.
* (c)   Reduce speed and overtake with caution.

Q. When you come up behind a vehicle which is going from side to side on the road in an unsafe manner, you should .....

Ans. * (a)   stay well back until the road widens sufficiently to allow you overtake safely.
    (b)   flash your lights and gesture aggressively at the other driver.
    (c)   drive close behind with a view to overtaking.

Q. A heavy goods vehicle has moved out in order to make a left turn up ahead. You should .....

Ans.   (a)   drive into the space on its left-hand side.
      * (b)   stay behind it and allow it to finish the turn.
         (c)   move out immediately and overtake as quickly as possible.

Q. A bus up ahead is signalling to make a left-hand turn and has moved out to make the turn. There is oncoming traffic. You should ......

Ans.   (a)   overtake on the left-hand-side.
         (b)   overtake on the right-hand-side.
      * (c)   stay back and allow the bus to complete the turn.

Q. When you see a truck reversing into a side entrance on the left-hand side up ahead, you should .....

Ans.   (a)   try to drive past it.
         (b)   sound your horn to indicate to the driver of the truck that you wish to overtake.
      * (c)   stop and wait until your way is clear.

Q.   You wish to turn right at traffic lights and the green light is on. There is oncoming traffic. You should .....

Ans. * (a)   go forward towards the centre of the junction and wait for a suitable gap to appear in the oncoming traffic before making the turn.

(b)   remain at the stop line until a suitable gap in the oncoming traffic appears before making the turn.

(c)   wait until a green arrow comes on.

Q.   Should you overtake a vehicle where you are liable to force oncoming traffic onto the hard shoulder on the opposite side of the road.

Ans.   (a)   Yes.

(b)   Yes, provided none of the oncoming traffic is overtaking.

* (c)   No.

Q.   Forcing oncoming traffic on to the hard shoulder on the opposite side of the road is considered to be .....

Ans.   (a)   safe driving.

* (b)   dangerous driving.

(c)   dangerous driving only at night.

Q. Can you move into the hard shoulder if there is oncoming traffic, to allow following traffic to overtake you?

Ans.   (a)   No.
    *   (b)   Yes.
        (c)   Only, if a truck or bus is oncoming.

Q. Can you drive on the hard shoulder in order to let faster moving traffic to overtake you?

Ans.   *   (a)   Yes.
        (b)   Only if driving on a dual-carriageway.
        (c)   Only if a truck or bus wishes to overtake you.

Q. In a queue of traffic which is being controlled by traffic lights, you should .....

Ans.   (a)   overtake on the right and move to the head of the queue.
    *   (b)   maintain your position in the queue.
        (c)   overtake on the left and move to the head of the queue.

Q. What effect could driving a smoother and more powerful car have on your sense of driving?

Ans. (a) It could make you feel the brakes appear more powerful than they actually are.

* (b) It could make you think that you are driving slower than you are actually driving.

(c) It could make you think that you are driving faster than you are actually driving.

Q. How can a smoother and more powerful motorbike affect your sense of perception?

Ans. (a) It could induce you to drive slower than you realise.

* (b) It could induce you to drive faster than you realise.

(c) It could induce you to think that you would be less likely to be affected by cross winds.

Q. You are riding a motorcycle and you wish to change lanes. You should firstly .....

Ans. * (a) use your mirrors and look around where necessary before indicating and moving over.

(b) use your indicators and move over.

(c) use your indicators and give a hand signal where necessary before moving over.

REACTION TIME

Q.   **Subject to the speed limit, the 'safest' speed at which to drive is .....**

Ans. * (a)   the speed which enables you to stop within the distance ahead which you can see to be clear.

        (b)   at the speed limit.

        (c)   the speed of other road users.

ATTENTION

Q.   **You are driving along and wish to use a hand held mobile phone. You should .....**

Ans.   (a)   steer with one hand.

    * (b)   stop at a safe location before using the phone.

        (c)   secure the phone between your shoulder and the side of your head while steering with both hands.

Q.   **You are stopped at traffic lights and the green light comes on. You should .....**

Ans.   (a)   accelerate quickly.

        (b)   check your mirrors.

    * (c)   check that other road users have cleared the junction, and move off with care.

PATIENCE

Q.   Which of the following should you do if another vehicle denies your right of way at a junction .....

Ans.   *   (a)   be patient.
          (b)   flash your lights to express your displeasure.
          (c)   go after the vehicle with the intention of complaining to the driver.

Q.   You are about to undertake a journey but are upset or angry about something. You should .....

Ans.   *   (a)   not drive until you are calm.
          (b)   try to relax as you drive along.
          (c)   drive faster than normal for a distance.

Q.   You are driving along and another vehicle is overtaking you. There is oncoming traffic. You should .....

Ans.   *   (a)   reduce speed and allow the other vehicle to move in in front of you.
          (b)   maintain your position because the other driver should not have attempted to overtake you.
          (c)   maintain your position and flash your lights to warn the oncoming traffic.

Q.   When in a hurry and another vehicle cuts
            into your path, you should .....

Ans. *   (a)   be patient and not retaliate.
          (b)   flash your lights to express your annoyance.
          (c)   drive faster to make up for lost time.

Q.   One of your tyres goes flat as you are driving
            along. You should .....

Ans. *   (a)   stop at a safe place and change the tyre.
          (b)   stop immediately and change the tyre.
          (c)   stop immediately, unless on a motorway, and
                   change the tyre.

Q.   You wish to change to the traffic lane on your
            right in which there is other traffic driving
            along. You should .....

Ans. *   (a)   use your mirror, signal, and move into the
                   right-hand lane when a suitable gap appears
                   in the traffic in that lane.
          (b)   indicate and move gradually into the right-
                   hand lane.
          (c)   pull in and stop, wait until a suitable gap
                   appears and then move out to the right-
                   hand lane.

ALCOHOL

Q.   **What effect can alcohol have on driving behaviour?**

Ans.   (a)   It can increase perception and awareness.
     *   (b)   It can contribute to a false sense of security and alertness.
          (c)   As long as the amount of alcohol consumed is within the prescribed legal limit, it does not affect driving behaviour.

Q.   **What effect does drinking alcohol have on a driver?**

Ans.   (a)   It increases awareness.
     *   (b)   It slows down the driver's ability to react.
          (c)   It has no effect.

MEDICATION

Q.   **You are taking medication which may affect your driving. You should .....**

Ans.   *   (a)   ask your doctor if you may drive.
          (b)   drink plenty of water while driving.
          (c)   drive for short distances only.

OBSERVANCE OF SAFE DISTANCE AND DRIVING IN VARIOUS WEATHER/ROAD CONDITIONS

SAFE DISTANCE/CLEARANCE

Q. **What effect does a wet road surface have on your vehicle's braking ability?**

Ans. * (a) It at least doubles the normal stopping distance which is required on a dry surface.

(b) It requires half as long again to stop as on a dry surface.

(c) It reduces the stopping distance required.

Q. **When driving uphill behind a slow-moving vehicle, you should .....**

Ans. (a) drive close behind it while keeping well to the left.

(b) drive close behind it while keeping to the centre of the road.

* (c) stay well behind until you can safely overtake it.

Q.   **After overtaking another vehicle, you should .....**

Ans.   (a)   cut into the left as soon as you have passed it.

*   (b)   check that you are well past the other vehicle before gradually moving into the left.

(c)   continue to signal right for a distance.

Q.   **What is the possible effect of cutting in too soon when overtaking another vehicle?**

Ans. * (a)   Both vehicles could collide.

(b)   The steering could lock.

(c)   The engine could lose power.

Q   **When you are overtaking parked vehicles, you should .....**

Ans. * (a)   allow sufficient clearance as you pass.

(b)   drive without care.

(c)   keep close to the vehicles and watch out for pedestrians.

Q.   **What stopping distance should you allow when you suspect that the road may be icy?**

Ans. * (a)   Up to 4 times the normal.

(b)   Up to 3 times the normal.

(c)   Twice the normal distance.

Q. What clearance should drivers normally allow for parked vehicles?

Ans. * (a) A door-width.
(b) The width of a mirror.
(c) A person-width.

Q. The recommended minimum gap per mile per hour which should be left between vehicles travelling on dry roads is .....

Ans. * (a) I metre for each mile per hour.
(b) I car length for each mile per hour.
(c) I0 metres for each mile per hour.

Q. You are riding a motor cycle and wish to overtake the car in front. You should .....

Ans. (a) rev your motorcycle engine loudly as a warning.
(b) attempt to overtake regardless of the circumstances.
* (c) wait until the opportunity presents itself to overtake safely.

ROADHOLDING

Q.   **Why does it take longer to stop the vehicle after heavy rain?**

Ans.   (a)   The brake fluid will be less effective in wet weather.

*   (b)   The tyres will have less road grip than in dry weather.

(c)   The suspension of the vehicle will be lighter in wet weather.

Q.   **Where there is a film of water between your vehicle's tyres and the road surface, the vehicle's .....**

Ans.   (a)   steering and braking will be more effective

(b)   braking will be more effective

*   (c)   steering and braking will be less effective.

Q.   **If you encounter loose chippings on a road, you should .....**

Ans.   (a)   press your hand against the windscreen or motorcycle faring.

(b)   increase speed so as to avoid causing damage to the vehicle.

*   (c)   slow down and allow extra clearance to all traffic until you have cleared the road works.

Q.   Spilled diesel on the road would .....

Ans * (a)   make the road more slippery.
      (b)   increase tyre noise.
      (c)   improve tyre grip on bends.

Q.   When driving in slippery road conditions, you should .....

Ans. * (a)   drive at lower speeds and use gentle acceleration and braking.
      (b)   apply the brakes sharply from time to time to test the road surface.
      (c)   drive at normal speed but allow extra stopping distance.

Q.   If the road is slippery should you drive your tractor with the left hand wheels up on the grass verge in order to improve roadholding?

Ans.   (a)   Yes.
   * (b)   No.
      (c)   Yes, if towing a trailer.

Q.   Why should you drive a tractor more slowly on uneven roads?

Ans.   (a)   To ensure that fuel does not spill from the tank.
   * (b)   To avoid severe bouncing.
      (c)   To reduce noise.

Q. When driving downhill on snow or ice, you should .....

Ans. (a) use a higher gear than normal in order to avoid wheelspin.

(b) keep close to the left and brake sharply to keep the speed down.

* (c) use a lower gear and brake gently to keep the speed down.

Q. How does driving at high speed affect your vehicle's road holding?

Ans. (a) The wheel alignment keeps the tyres in full contact with the road.

(b) The suspension compensates for any unevenness in the road surface.

* (c) The road holding ability of the vehicle is reduced.

Q. Should the handbrake be used to bring the vehicle to a halt?

Ans. * (a) No.

(b) Yes.

(c) Only at speeds below 5 m.p.h..

Q. If you apply the handbrake while the vehicle is moving at speed .....

Ans.   (a)   the A.B.S. could disconnect.
   * (b)   the back wheels could lock causing the vehicle to skid.
      (c)   the vehicle could not skid.

STOPPING DISTANCE AND BRAKING ABILITY

Q. The normal stopping distance of a car travelling at 30 m.p.h. on a dry road is .....

Ans.   (a)   15 metres.
      (b)   20 metres.
   * (c)   23 metres.

Q. The normal stopping distance of a car travelling at 30 m.p.h. on a wet road is.....

Ans.   (a)   20 metres.
   * (b)   30 metres.
      (c)   40 metres.

Q. The normal stopping distance of a car travelling at 60 m.p.h. on a dry road is.....

Ans. * (a)   72 metres.
      (b)   62 metres.
      (c)   52 metres.

Q. The normal stopping distance of a car travelling at 60 m.p.h. on a wet road is.....

Ans.   (a)   100 metres.
        (b)   90 metres.
    * (c)   124 metres.

Q. What danger can arise if you have to brake suddenly?

Ans. * (a)   The vehicle behind might run into the back of your vehicle.
        (b)   Your vehicle's braking system could lose a lot of air or fluid.
        (c)   Your vehicle's braking system could overheat.

Q. Which of the following does not affect braking distance?

Ans.   (a)   The speed and weight of the vehicle.
        (b)   Road conditions and the tyres on the vehicle.
    * (c)   The power of the engine.

Q. Two vehicles each travelling at 50 m.p.h. collide head-on. What would be the combined speed at impact?

Ans. * (a)   100 m.p.h.
        (b)   200 m.p.h.
        (c)   50 m.p.h.

Q.   In order to judge a safe distance to drive
         behind the vehicle in front, you should .....

Ans. * (a)   allow at least 2 seconds to elapse between
                   the vehicle in front and your vehicle passing
                   a fixed point.
            (b)   check your speedometer.
            (c)   allow at least 3 vehicle lengths for each mile
                   per hour between the vehicles.

Q.   What effect does carrying a load have on
         your vehicle's braking ability?

Ans. * (a)   It increases the distance required to stop.
            (b)   It reduces the distance required to stop.
            (c)   It has no effect provided the brakes are in
                   good condition.

Q.   If two vehicles each travelling at 40 m.p.h.
         collide head-on, the speed on impact is .....

Ans.   (a)   40 m.p.h.
            (b)   60 m.p.h.
         * (c)   80 m.p.h.

Q.   If two vehicles each travelling at 60 m.p.h.
         collide head-on, the speed on impact is .....

Ans.   (a)   60 m.p.h.
            (b)   100 m.p.h.
         * (c)   120 m.p.h.

Q. **What effect does towing a loaded trailer have on stopping ability?**

Ans. (a) It significantly reduces stopping distance.
* (b) It significantly increases stopping distance.
(c) It has no effect.

DRIVING RISK FACTORS RELATED TO VARIOUS ROAD CONDITIONS, IN PARTICULAR AS THEY CHANGE WITH THE WEATHER AND THE TIME OF DAY OR NIGHT.

DRIVING IN FOG

Q.   **When you are driving in dense fog, you should .....**

Ans.   *   (a)   drive slowly on dipped headlights.

           (b)   drive on sidelights only.

           (c)   drive on sidelights and hazard warning lights.

Q.   **When you are driving in dense fog, you should .....**

Ans.   (a)   drive along the central dividing line and watch for the reflective studs.

           (b)   switch on your full headlights and drive slowly.

      *   (c)   drive slowly on your dipped headlights.

Q.   **Rear fog lamps should be used .....**

Ans.   (a)   always when driving at night.

           (b)   when the vehicle behind is too close.

      *   (c)   only in fog.

Q. When may you drive your vehicle showing a high intensity fog light to the rear?

Ans.   (a)   When the tail-light is broken.
     * (b)   In fog, heavy rain, or snow.
      (c)   Never.

DRIVING AT NIGHT

Q. Incorrectly aimed headlights could .....

Ans.   (a)   cause the headlights to overheat.
      (b)   reduce the wattage of the headlights.
     * (c)   dazzle oncoming road users and reduce their visibility.

Q. Driving at night, you should dip your headlights when .....

Ans.   (a)   approaching a bend or the brow of a hill.
      (b)   driving at less than 30 m.p.h.
     * (c)   meeting or driving behind other traffic, or in a lit-up area.

Q. If you are blinded by the lights of an oncoming vehicle, you should .....

Ans.   (a)   reduce speed and switch on your full headlights.
      (b)   drive well to the left and maintain your speed.
     * (c)   slow down and stop if necessary.

Q. **You have been driving regularly in daylight and must now undertake a journey at night. You should .....**

Ans. (a) drive at a higher speed than during the day as traffic is lighter at night.

(b) drive at the same speed as during the day.

* (c) drive at a slower speed than in the day as visibility is reduced at night.

Q. **When driving at night, you should .....**

Ans. (a) increase your speed as traffic is lighter at night.

(b) turn up the radio volume to help maintain your concentration.

* (c) drive at a speed which will enable you to stop within the distance which you can see to be clear.

Q. **When driving at night, which of the following is the safest approach to adopt?**

Ans. (a) Drive with full headlights at all times.

* (b) Drive at a speed which allows you to stop within the distance which you can see to be clear.

(c) Drive with dipped headlights at all times.

Q.   **When meeting an oncoming vehicle at night, you should .....**

Ans.   (a)   focus your eyes directly on its lights.
*   (b)   not look directly at its lights.
(c)   look down at the dash until it has passed so as not to be dazzled by its lights.

Q.   **When may you drive with full headlights in a built up area at night?**

Ans.   * (a)   Never.
(b)   When there is no oncoming traffic.
(c)   Between the hours of 11.30 p.m. and 7.00 a.m.

Q.   **What lights should you have on when driving close behind other traffic at night?**

Ans.   * (a)   Dipped headlights.
(b)   Full headlights.
(c)   Sidelights.

Q.   **You must dip your headlights when .....**

Ans.   * (a)   meeting or driving behind other vehicles or in lit-up areas.
(b)   driving at less than 30 m.p.h..
(c)   approaching a bend or the brow of a hill.

Q.   **When driving late at night what should you be aware of?**

Ans.

    (a)   That reflectorised studs will warn you of bends ahead.

* (b)   The danger of falling asleep.

    (c)   Speed limits do not apply between midnight and 6 a.m.

Q.   **If you are dazzled by the lights of an oncoming vehicle at night, you should .....**

Ans.

    (a)   turn your head to one side.

    (b)   shield your eyes with your hand.

* (c)   slow down and do not look directly at the lights of the oncoming vehicle.

Q.   **If you are dazzled by headlights reflecting in the rear view mirror of your car, you should .....**

Ans.

    (a)   turn on your rear fog lights to signal to the following driver to turn off his headlights.

* (b)   adjust the night driving mode on your mirror.

    (c)   adjust your mirror to reflect the light back towards the following driver.

Q. **What would you do if dazzled by lights reflecting in your mirror?**

Ans. (a) Adjust your mirror to reflect the light back to the following driver.

(b) Switch on your rear lights.

* (c) Temporarily adjust the angle of your mirror.

Q. **When driving a car at night, what effect could driving with a single headlight have on oncoming drivers?**

Ans. (a) It could enable them to see your vehicle more clearly.

(b) It could dazzle them more.

* (c) They could mistake your vehicle for a motorcycle.

Q. **Generally, what lighting must a car, tractor or works vehicle have when driving at night?**

Ans. * (a) Headlights, side lights front and rear, rear number plate light, red rear reflectors, brake lights and indicators.

(b) Headlights only.

(c) Headlights and a reversing light.

Q. The lighting requirements for a motor-cycle at night are .....

Ans. * (a) headlight, red rear light, a number plate light and a red rear reflector.

(b) brake light and a headlight.

(c) indicators, a brake light and a headlight.

Q. When driving at night you see a single headlight approaching from ahead. You should .....

Ans. (a) carry on because it can only be a motorcycle.

(b) switch on your high beams as a warning.

* (c) keep well to the left in case it is a four wheeled-vehicle.

Q. What lights must your motorcycle show when parked at night on an unlit road.

Ans. * (a) A white light to the front and red light to the rear.

(b) No lights are required.

(c) Dipped headlight and a red parking light to the rear.

Q. When parking your car, tractor or work vehicle at night on an unlit public road, what lights must it show?

Ans. * (a) At least one side-lamp front and rear on the side nearest the centre of the road.
(b) No lights are required.
(c) Dipped head lights.

DRIVING ON SLIPPERY SURFACES

Q. When driving on an icy road, you should .....

Ans. (a) drive in a low gear at all times.
(b) drive at normal speed but apply the brakes from time to time to check for grip.
* (c) drive at a slower speed than usual using gentle acceleration and braking.

Q. When driving a vehicle, what effect could icy roads have?

Ans. * (a) The vehicle could skid more easily than normal.
(b) Tyre grip could improve.
(c) Tyre treads could wear out more rapidly.

Q. When driving in slippery road conditions, you should .....

Ans. (a) accelerate harder using the lower gears.

(b) apply the brakes regularly in order to improve tyre grip.

* (c) use gentle acceleration through all the gears.

Q. How should you negotiate a bend when the road is slippery?

Ans. (a) Press the clutch and brake together.

(b) Accelerate sharply.

* (c) Drive slowly and smoothly.

Q. Apart from the risk of skidding, what danger may arise when driving in snow?

Ans. * (a) You may not be able to see road signs and markings clearly.

(b) The vehicle's exhaust may be rapidly cooled by spray or mud.

(c) Moisture in the vehicle's air tanks may freeze.

Q. When driving in heavy rain, you should .....

Ans. * (a) beware of aquaplaning.

(b) maintain normal speeds as on a dry road.

(c) weave the vehicle slightly from side to side in order to improve tyre-grip.

Q.   What is the danger in driving with badly worn tyres at high speed on wet roads?

Ans. * (a)   You have less control over your vehicle because it is gliding on a film of water.

(b)   Air pressure in the tyres is reduced.

(c)   There is no danger provided the tyres are at the correct pressure.

Q.   When you encounter mud on the road, you should .....

Ans. (a)   apply the brakes immediately.

(b)   change to a lower gear and carry on.

* (c)   reduce speed gradually while keeping a look out for tractors or earthmoving machines.

DRIVING ON A FLOODED ROAD

Q.   You have just driven through a flooded part of the road. You should .....

Ans. (a)   drive faster for a time in order to dry out your brakes.

(b)   apply the brakes firmly to check if they are still effective.

* (c)   press the brake pedal lightly at slow speed for a short distance in order to dry your brakes.

Q. How would wet weather affect your vehicle's engine performance?

Ans.
    (a)   It would reduce the power output.
    (b)   It would cause it to run at higher temperatures.
* (c)   It would have no effect.

Q. When you come to a part of the road which is flooded, you should .....

Ans.
    (a)   increase speed in order to get through it quickly.
* (b)   reduce speed, and use a lower gear.
    (c)   use a high gear and maintain your speed.

DRIVING IN WINDY CONDITIONS

Q. How could strong winds affect a motorcyclist?

Ans.
    (a)   They would have no effect provided the bike was driven slowly.
* (b)   They could blow the motorcyclist off course.
    (c)   They would only cause instability on exposed stretches of road.

ROADWORKS

Q. When you are driving along and see road-works up ahead, you should .....

Ans. * (a) reduce speed and be prepared to stop for earthmoving machinery or a flagman.

(b) engage a lower gear to improve grip and maintain your speed.

(c) increase speed in order to avoid getting stuck in soft ground.

Q. When you see roadworks up ahead, you should be aware that .....

Ans. * (a) there may be mud or chippings on the road.

(b) traffic is likely to travel much faster.

(c) you have right of way over earthmoving machinery.

HUMP-BACKED BRIDGE

Q. What should you be aware of when driving a tractor over a hump-backed bridge while towing a trailer?

Ans. (a) Tail-swing.

* (b) The trailer could become detached if a severe bump is encountered at speed.

(c) The tractor's suspension will smooth out the bump.

CHARACTERISTICS OF VARIOUS TYPES OF ROAD.

ONE-WAY STREET

Q.   You are driving in a one-way street and you wish to turn right. You should drive close to .....

Ans.   (a)   the centre line of the road.

(b)   the left-hand-side of the road.

* (c)   the right-hand-side of the road.

Q.   When you are on a one-way street and wish to turn right up ahead, you should .....

Ans.   (a)   drive on the left until you are close to the turn before taking up position on the right.

* (b)   move to the right hand side in good time.

(c)   drive close to the centre of the road.

BUS LANE

Q.   When you wish to turn left into your driveway and there is a bus lane on your left, you should .....

Ans.   (a)   use a 'slowing down' hand signal in addition to your left turn indicator.

* (b)   watch out for cyclists, taxis and buses which may be using the lane.

(c)   watch out for buses only.

Q. **When may you drive in a 'contra-flow' bus lane?**

Ans. (a) After lighting-up time.
   * (b) Never.
      (c) When the regular bus service is finished.

Q. **What traffic may use a 'contra-flow' bus lane?**

Ans. (a) Buses, taxis and cyclists.
   * (b) Buses on a scheduled service.
      (c) Buses and taxis.

Q. **What traffic may use a 'with-flow' bus lane during the specified times?**

Ans. (a) Buses only.
      (b) All traffic.
   * (c) Buses on a scheduled service, taxis and cyclists.

Q. **When may you drive in a 'with-flow' bus lane?**

Ans. (a) During the hours specified on the bus lane information plate.
   * (b) Outside the hours specified on the bus lane information plate.
      (c) After a bus has gone through on it.

DUAL-CARRIAGEWAY

Q.   When you are driving along on a dual-carriageway, you should normally .....

Ans.
- (a)   drive on the right-hand lane.
- (b)   drive on either lane of your choice.
- * (c)   drive on the left-hand lane unless you wish to overtake, or turn right.

Q.   When you wish to turn right from a minor road onto a dual-carriageway which has a wide median strip, you should .....

Ans.
- (a)   not drive onto the dual-carriageway until there is a suitable gap in the traffic from both directions.
- * (b)   drive onto the median strip when the nearest carriageway is clear and then wait for a gap in traffic from the left, before proceeding.
- (c)   not turn right onto a dual-carriagaeway.

Q.   When you wish to turn right on to a dual-carriageway which has a narrow median strip, you should .....

Ans. *
- (a)   wait on the side road until there is a suitable gap in the traffic from both directions.
- (b)   when the nearest carriageway is clear, drive on to the median strip and wait.
- (c)   you are not allowed to turn right onto a dual-carriageway.

MOTORWAY

Q.   **When driving on a motorway or dual-carriageway, you should .....**

Ans.   (a)   relax because there will be no oncoming or crossing traffic.
   *   (b)   be alert for other drivers who may suddenly change lanes or reduce speed.
   (c)   match your speed to that of the vehicle in front.

Q.   **When driving on a motorway, you should .....**

Ans.   *   (a)   drive in the left-hand lane unless you intend to overtake.
   (b)   drive on whichever lane has the least volume of traffic.
   (c)   not drive on the left-hand lane as it is reserved for heavy goods vehicles and coaches.

Q.   **When driving on a motorway, you should .....**

Ans.   (a)   relax because there will be no oncoming or crossing traffic.
   (b)   match your speed to that of the vehicle in front.
   *   (c)   be alert for other drivers who may suddenly change lanes or reduce speed.

Q.   **When driving on a motorway, you should .....**

Ans.   (a)   increase tyre pressure in order to cope with sustained high speeds.

         (b)   reduce tyre pressure because high speeds will cause them to heat up.

     *   (c)   ensure tyre pressure is normal.

Q.   **When you wish to join a motorway from a slip road, you should .....**

Ans.   *   (a)   try to match your speed to that of traffic already on the motorway and merge into it in a suitable gap.

         (b)   drive directly onto the motorway.

         (c)   drive along the hard shoulder if necessary until a suitable gap appears in the motorway traffic to allow you to merge with it.

Q.   **When may you pick up or set down a passenger on a motorway?**

Ans.   (a)   When you stop on the hard-shoulder.

     *   (b)   Never.

         (c)   When you are within 200 metres of a slip-road.

Q. When driving on a motorway and you wish to turn back, you should .....

Ans.   (a)   cross to the opposite side of the motorway when there is a suitable gap in the oncoming traffic.

        (b)   wait on the hard shoulder until a suitable gap appears in traffic from both directions and then cross to the opposite side of the motorway.

*   (c)   carry on to the next available slip road and cross the motorway by means of the fly over.

Q. On leaving a motorway, you should .....

Ans.   (a)   reduce speed gradually for a few miles.

        (b)   maintain your speed until traffic conditions oblige you to slow down.

*   (c)   comply with the speed limit on the road you are joining.

Q. If you drive past your intended exit on a motorway, you should .....

Ans.   (a)   stop on the hard shoulder and reverse back to the exit.

        (b)   use the emergency telephone to ask for advice.

*   (c)   drive on to the next exit.

Q.   **Of the following, what is the difference between driving on a motorway and driving on other types of road?**

Ans.   *   (a)   Traffic usually travels at higher speed on a motorway.
                (b)   Handsignals may not be used on a motorway.
                (c)   Speed limits are the same for all vehicles on a motorway.

Q.   **When you are driving on a motorway and wish to overtake another vehicle, you should .....**

Ans.   (a)   use the mirror, signal and overtake in the left-hand lane if necessary.
                (b)   check for following traffic and overtake in either lane.
            *   (c)   use the mirror, signal and overtake in the right-hand lane.

Q.   **On exiting a motorway, you should .....**

Ans.   (a)   maintain motorway speeds for a few miles.
            *   (b)   be alert for oncoming and crossing traffic.
                (c)   not overtake for a few miles.

Q.   **On leaving a motorway, you should .....**

Ans.   (a)   reduce speed gradually for a few miles.
                (b)   drive up to 70 miles per hour.
            *   (c)   obey the reduced speed limit.

ROADS OF EQUAL IMPORTANCE

Q. When you are are coming to a junction where the roads are of equal importance and you wish to go straight ahead, you should .....

Ans.
    (a) carry on as normal because you have the right of way.
* (b) give way to traffic coming from your right.
    (c) give way to traffic coming from your left.

Q. When approaching a junction where the roads are of equal importance, you should .....

Ans.
    (a) give way to all the traffic at the junction.
* (b) give way to traffic approaching from your right.
    (c) give way to trucks and buses only.

CLEARWAY

Q. What is a clearway?

Ans. * (a) A road where stopping and parking is prohibited during certain periods.
    (b) A road which is reserved for pedestrians only.
    (c) A road which is reserved for buses only.

FACING DOWNHILL

Q. **When you wish to park facing downhill, you should .....**

Ans.

    (a)   angle your wheels towards the road.

*   (b)   angle your wheels towards the kerb.

    (c)   angle your wheels in the straight ahead position.

UNMARKED ROAD

Q. **When you are driving on a road which is not marked by a central dividing line, you should .....**

Ans.

    (a)   drive on the middle of the road.

    (b)   imagine there is one there and drive on the right-hand side.

*   (c)   imagine there is one there and drive on the left-hand side.

NARROW ROAD

Q. **When you are driving on a narrow road and approaching a sharp bend, you should .....**

Ans. * (a)   reduce speed, keep well to the left and watch for oncoming traffic.

    (b)   maintain your speed and flash your lights as a warning.

    (c)   wait until you are close to the bend before braking.

ROUNDABOUTS

Q.   As you approach a roundabout, you should .....

Ans.   (a)   drive onto it as the traffic on it must give way to you.

       * (b)   give way to traffic already on the roundabout.

       (c)   give way only to heavy goods vehicles on the roundabout.

Q.   In which direction do you drive around a roundabout?

Ans.   *   (a)   Left.

       (b)   Right.

       (c)   Left or right.

Q.   You are on a two-lane approach to a roundabout and wish to turn right. What lane should you use?

Ans.   *   (a)   The right-hand lane.

       (b)   The left-hand lane.

       (c)   Either lane.

Q. When you are coming to a roundabout and you wish to turn left, you should .....

Ans.
    (a)   approach in any lane and give a clear signal.

    (b)   approach in the right hand lane and give way to traffic which is already on the roundabout.

*   (c)   approach in the left-hand lane and give way to traffic which is already on the roundabout.

Q. You wish to take the second exit at a roundabout. What signals should you give?

Ans.
    (a)   Give no signals.

    (b)   Signal to the left as you approach the roundabout.

*   (c)   Give no signal on the approach, then signal left as you pass the exit before the one you wish to take.

Q. You are stopped at a roundabout. Which of these factors is the most important in deciding whether or not to proceed?

Ans.
    (a)   The distance to the road from which you intend to leave the roundabout.

*   (b)   The distance and speed of the traffic coming from the right.

    (c)   The distance and speed of traffic coming from behind.

TURNING RIGHT

Q.   **Which of the following is the correct road position for a vehicle when turning right?**

Ans.   (a)   The left-hand side of the road.

             (b)   The right-hand side of the road.

     *   (c)   Just left of the centre of the road.

Q.   **When you are driving on a main road and intend to turn right into a minor road, you should .....**

Ans. *   (a)   yield right-of-way to oncoming traffic and to pedestrians who may be crossing at the junction.

             (b)   turn in front of oncoming traffic as it must give right-of-way to you.

             (c)   stop and allow other traffic to exit from the minor road.

VULNERABLE ROAD USERS

ALLOWING SUFFICIENT TIME FOR OTHERS

Q.   **When you are approaching a junction where a pedestrian is walking across the road, you should .....**

Ans.   *   (a)   yield right-of-way to the pedestrian.

(b)   sound the horn as a warning of your approach.

(c)   carry on because the pedestrian only has right-of-way at a pedestrian crossing.

Q.   **When you are being delayed for the time being by a cyclist just ahead, you should .....**

Ans.   (a)   try to squeeze past the cyclist despite oncoming traffic.

(b)   drive close behind to encourage the cyclist to pull in.

*   (c)   stay well back until you have an opportunity to overtake safely.

Q. When you are stopped at traffic lights and the green light is about to come on as pedestrians are crossing the road, you should .....

Ans. * (a) wait as long as is necessary to enable them to complete the crossing.

(b) sound the horn as a warning to them that the lights are about to change.

(c) inch forward in your vehicle to encourage them to complete the crossing quickly.

Q. When you are following a car which is being driven by an elderly or disabled driver, you should be aware that .....

Ans. (a) the driver is not required to use indicators.

(b) the driver does not have to obey the parking restrictions.

* (c) the driver's reactions may be slower than normal.

Q. You see a vehicle up ahead which is being driven slowly by a learner driver. You should .....

Ans. (a) quickly overtake the vehicle to avoid being delayed.

* (b) be patient and allow extra time to the driver if necessary.

(c) drive close behind the vehicle to encourage the driver to speed up.

Q. The vehicle in front of you is being driven by a learner driver and is causing an obstruction. You should .....

Ans. * (a) stay back and allow the driver to proceed at his/her own speed.

(b) sound the horn to encourage the driver to pull in.

(c) drive close behind the vehicle in front and flash your headlights.

Q. An inexperienced learner driver is in traffic situations more likely to react .....

Ans. (a) more quickly.

* (b) more slowly.

(c) more correctly.

Q. You see a cyclist just ahead who is about to overtake a parked vehicle. There is oncoming traffic. You should .....

Ans. (a) expect the cyclist to go on the inside of the vehicle.

(b) allow enough clearance to overtake both the parked vehicle and the cyclist together.

* (c) allow the cyclist to overtake the parked vehicle, and then proceed.

Q. When you are driving in slow-moving traffic in a built up area and there is a pedestrian crossing up ahead, you should .....

Ans. (a) stop your vehicle on the pedestrian crossing if necessary.

(b) drive close up behind the vehicle in front and move forward when it moves.

* (c) time your stop/start movements to avoid obstructing the pedestrian crossing.

REDUCING SPEED HAVING REGARD TO OTHER ROAD USERS

Q. When you see an elderly person crossing the road up ahead, you should .....

Ans. (a) increase your speed to pass quickly.

* (b) reduce your speed sufficiently to enable the person to complete the crossing safely.

(c) increase your engine noise to warn the person of your approach.

Q. While driving at 50 m.p.h. you see some children on the road up ahead.
You should .....

Ans. (a) turn on your headlights.

(b) maintain your speed.

* (c) reduce speed and prepare to stop if necessary.

CLEARANCE

Q.   **What should you do when you see children just ahead on the road?**

Ans. *   (a)   Give them a wide clearance and be prepared to slow down if necessary.
          (b)   Keep your course as the noise of the engine will make them keep in.
          (c)   Flash your lights to warn them of your presence.

Q.   **If while driving on a windy day you see a cyclist ahead of you, you should .....**

Ans. *   (a)   allow extra clearance in case the cyclist is blown off course.
          (b)   expect the cyclist to be alert and to keep in to the left.
          (c)   maintain your course but prepare to swerve around the cyclist if necessary.

Q.   **When you are overtaking a cyclist, you should .....**

Ans.   (a)   sound the horn as a warning.
          *   (b)   allow extra clearance in case the cyclist swerves suddenly.
          (c)   drive close to the cyclist and overtake promptly.

Q. When you see joggers up ahead on the left, you should .....

Ans. * (a) use your mirrors, indicate, and overtake allowing sufficient clearance.

(b) sound the horn to warn them to move in or stop.

(c) expect them to move in so that you can pass them by.

Q. If you are driving on a road which has a potholed surface and there is a cyclist up ahead, you should .....

Ans. * (a) allow extra clearance in case the cyclist swerves out to avoid a pothole.

(b) maintain your course and sound your horn to alert the cyclist of your approach.

(c) expect the cyclist to keep to the left and maintain your speed.

ANTICIPATION OF VULNERABLE ROAD USERS

Q. What precautions should you take in relation to pedestrians when driving in slow-moving traffic?

Ans. (a) Allow them to cross the road only at pedestrian crossings.

* (b) Watch for pedestrians who may cross the road in front of your vehicle.

(c) Do not leave a gap between your vehicle and the vehicle in front.

Q.   **What precautions should you take in relation to pedestrians when driving in slow moving traffic?**

Ans.   (a)   Sound your horn occasionally as a warning.
            (b)   Rev your engine occasionally as a warning.
    *   (c)   Look around and check your mirrors regularly.

Q.   **What should you be aware of when making a left-hand turn?**

Ans.   *   (a)   Cyclists might come up on the 'inside'.
                 (b)   That following traffic has room to overtake.
                 (c)   That you approach with the nearside wheels close against the kerb.

Q.   **When driving through a housing estate in daylight/during the day, you should .....**

Ans.   (a)   drive on the centre of the road.
            (b)   switch on your headlights to warn of your approach.
    *   (c)   anticipate the possibility of children or other residents coming out suddenly onto the road.

Q. When you approach a play area up ahead, you should .....

Ans. * (a) watch out for children who might suddenly dash onto the road.
  (b) obey the speed limit and maintain your course.
  (c) switch on your hazard warning lights.

Q. When making a left turn into a side road, you should .....

Ans. * (a) check for pedestrians or cyclists who may have come up on the 'inside'.
  (b) ensure that following traffic has room to overtake if necessary.
  (c) expect that traffic coming out of the other road will always stay back and allow you space.

Q. You are driving on a country road without footpaths. What should you look out for coming towards you on your side of the road?

Ans. (a) Motorcycles.
  * (b) Pedestrians.
  (c) Tractors.

Q. When you are driving at night on an unlit road, you should .....

Ans.
    (a)   maintain your speed when meeting oncoming traffic.

    (b)   drive on the centre of the road.

 * (c)   anticipate that there may be pedestrians up ahead who may be wearing dark clothing.

Q. What could happen if you park on a footpath?

Ans.
    (a)   The suspension could be weakened.

    (b)   The tyres could lose air pressure.

 * (c)   Pedestrians could be impeded.

SIGNALLING TO OTHER DRIVERS

Q. When you are driving along and see a cyclist on the road up ahead, you should .....

Ans. * (a)   use your mirrors, indicate in good time, and move out if safe to do so.

    (b)   use your mirrors, and move out to overtake without indicating.

    (c)   indicate, move out and check the mirror for following traffic.

Q. If indicators are not fitted or are not working, how should signals be given?

Ans.   (a)   It is not necessary to give signals provided you look around.

         (b)   Your position on the road is a signal in itself.

   *   (c)   By hand, clearly and in good time.

Q. There is traffic behind you while driving on an open road. If you meet a pedestrian, you should .....

Ans.   (a)   not signal.

         (b)   flash your lights at the pedestrian.

   *   (c)   signal to following traffic that you are about to overtake.

NECESSARY DOCUMENTS

DRIVING LICENCE AND PROVISIONAL DRIVING LICENCE MATTERS

Q. **What drivers are required to display 'L' Plates on their vehicles?**

Ans. (a)   Drivers on their second provisional licence.

(b)   Learner drivers who are accompanied by the holder of a "full" licence in the relevant vehicle category.

* (c)   All provisional licence holders except those driving motorcycles, agricultural tractors and works vehicles.

Q. **You have passed your test on a vehicle with automatic transmission. What restriction does this put on your licence?**

Ans. (a)   You may not drive at speeds of more than 50 m.p.h..

(b)   You must continue to display 'L' plates.

* (c)   You may not drive vehicles with manual transmission.

Q.   **What roads can provisionally licensed drivers drive on?**

Ans.   (a)   All roads.

    *   (b)   All roads except motorways.

    (c)   All roads except motorways and dual-carriageways.

Q.   **"L" Plates should be .....**

Ans.   (a)   a green "L" on a white background.

    (b)   a red "L" on a transparent background.

    *   (c)   a red "L" on a white background.

Q.   **"L" plates should be displayed on cars .....**

Ans.   (a)   on the front only.

    (b)   on the rear only.

    *   (c)   both front and rear.

Q.   **What roads are provisional licence holders not allowed to drive on?**

Ans.   (a)   National primary roads.

    *   (b)   Motorways.

    (c)   Dual-carriageways.

Q.   As a provisionally licensed car driver, you must be accompanied by a qualified driver during .....

Ans.   (a)   the term of your first provisional licence only.

    (b)   the term of your second and subsequent provisional licences.

* (c)   the terms of your first, third and subsequent provisional licences.

Q.   A provisionally licensed car driver must display 'L plates' on the vehicle .....

Ans. * (a)   at all times.

    (b)   while driving unaccompanied by a qualified driver.

    (c)   during the term of the driver's first provisional licence only.

Q.   What Provisional Licence holders are always exempt from having to be accompanied by qualified drivers?

Ans.   (a)   None.

    (b)   All.

* (c)   Provisional Licence holders in categories 'A', 'A1' and 'M'.

Q.　　When may a provisionally licensed motorcyclist carry a pillion passenger?

Ans.　　(a)　When the passenger holds a 'full' motorcycle licence.
　*　(b)　Never.
　　(c)　When the driver is over 25 years of age.

Q.　　What is the maximum engine capacity which the holder of a category A1 licence may drive?

Ans.　　(a)　250 c.c.
　　(b)　100 c.c.
　*　(c)　125 c.c.

Q.　　What is the maximum engine capacity which the holder of a category M licence may drive?

Ans.　*　(a)　50 c.c.
　　(b)　55 c.c.
　　(c)　65 c.c.

Q.　　What is the maximum kilometre speed per hour motorcycle which a category M licence holder may drive?

Ans.　　(a)　65 km/h
　　(b)　55 km/h
　*　(c)　45 km/h

Q. May the holder of a category A, A1 or M provisional licence or driving licence drive a tricycle or quadricycle ?

Ans.   (a)   Yes.
*   (b)   No.
  (c)   Yes, with a driving licence only.

Q. What is maximum engine power which a motorcyclist with a category A licence for less than 2 years may drive?

Ans.   (a)   11 kilowatts.
*   (b)   25 kilowatts.
  (c)   35 kilowatts.

Q. For how many years is a category A licence holder restricted to driving motorcycles with a maximum engine power of 25 kilowatts?

Ans.   (a)   1.
*   (b)   2.
  (c)   3.

Q. A motorcyclist who wishes to drive a motorcycle with a power maximum greater than 11 kilowatts must hold which category licence?

Ans.   (a)   M.
  (b)   A1.
*   (c)   A.

Q. What is the maximum engine power which a motorcyclist with a category A1 licence may drive?

Ans. * (a) 11 kilowatts.
(b) 15 kilowatts.
(c) 25 kilowatts.

Q. What is the maximum design gross vehicle weight which the holder of a category **B** licence may drive?

Ans. * (a) 3,500 kilogrammes.
(b) 2,500 kilogrammes.
(c) 4,500 kilogrammes.

Q. The holder of a category **B** provisional licence is not required to be accompanied by the holder of a "full" licence during the term of his/her .....

Ans. (a) first provisional licence.
* (b) second provisional licence.
(c) third provisional licence.

Q. What is the maximum number of passengers which the holder of a category **B** licence may carry in a vehicle?

Ans. (a) 10.
(b) 9.
* (c) 8.

Q. **A category W provisional licence holder may not carry a passenger unless .....**

Ans. (a) such person holds a category W driving licence.

   * (b) such person holds a category W driving licence and the vehicle is constructed or adapted to carry a passenger.

    (c) such person holds a category D driving licence and the vehicle is constructed or adapted to carry a passenger

VEHICLE REGISTRATION AND TAX REQUIREMENTS

Q. **May you use your vehicle in a public place when it does not have a current tax disc displayed?**

Ans. (a) Yes, but for not more than one month after the expiry of your previous disc.

    (b) Yes, but for not more than 10 days after the expiry of your previous disc.

   * (c) No.

Q. **What documents must you furnish when renewing your Motor Tax?**

Ans. (a) An application form.

    (b) An application form, the appropriate fee and your old tax disc.

   * (c) The Vehicle Registration book or the Vehicle Licensing Certificate (as appropriate), your current Insurance Certificate, and an application form.

Q. You wish to drive a vehicle and the tax disc is out of date. You should .....

Ans.
(a) notify the Gardai.
(b) renew it within 10 days of expiry.
* (c) not drive it.

Q. You wish to drive another vehicle which is not currently taxed. May you transfer the tax disc from your own vehicle onto it?

Ans.
(a) Yes, on a temporary basis.
(b) Yes, provided your own vehicle is not being used at the same time.
* (c) No.

Q. Who should ensure that the correct tax disc is displayed on a vehicle?

Ans.
(a) The driver, where not the owner.
* (b) The driver and owner are equally responsible.
(c) The owner, where not the driver.

Q. When must a current tax disc be displayed on a vehicle on a public road?

Ans.
(a) Not later than 3 months after registration.
(b) Not later than 6 months after registration.
* (c) At all times.

Q.   **Who may demand to see your vehicle registration document or vehicle licensing certificate, whichever applies in your case?**

Ans.   (a)   Any person with whom you are involved in an accident.

(b)   Any Traffic Warden.

*   (c)   Any member of the Gardai.

INSURANCE

Q.   **You are driving a vehicle which is not your own but with the owner's consent. Who is responsible for ensuring that the vehicle in question is properly insured?**

Ans.   (a)   The driver only.

*   (b)   Both the driver and the vehicle owner.

(c)   The vehicle owner only.

Q.   **Your insurance policy has expired. Are you still covered to drive your vehicle?**

Ans.   (a)   Yes, up to 10 days after expiry.

*   (b)   No.

(c)   Yes, up to 30 days after expiry.

Q. When you wish to drive another privately owned vehicle but you are uncertain if you are insured to drive it, you should .....

Ans. (a) transfer the insurance disc from your own vehicle on to it.

* (b) enquire from your own insurance company if you are covered to drive it.

(c) drive it provided you tell your insurance company within 10 days, and agree to pay any additional premium.

Q. When you wish to drive a vehicle and you are not sure if you are covered by insurance, you should .....

Ans. * (a) not drive until cover is confirmed by your insurance company.

(b) check with your local motor taxation office.

(c) check with your local Garda station.

Q. What is the minimum insurance cover which is required to drive a vehicle on a public road?

Ans. (a) Personal accident.

(b) Comprehensive.

* (c) Third-party.

Q. You are required to give the following details when you wish to obtain insurance cover on your vehicle .....

Ans. (a) all information relating to the previous 5 years.

(b) your age and details of your driving licence.

* (c) all information requested by the insurance company.

Q. When you have had the engine capacity of your vehicle altered, you should .....

Ans. (a) not exceed 30 m.p.h. for the first 1,000 miles after having the alteration made.

* (b) inform your local motor taxation office and your insurance company.

(c) inform your insurance company.

Q. Which of the following must be displayed on a vehicle's windscreen at all times?

Ans. (a) The insurance cover note.

* (b) The insurance disc.

(c) The insurance certificate.

AUTOMATIC TRANSMISSION

Q. You have passed your test on a vehicle with automatic transmission. You may drive .....

Ans. (a) all vehicles in the licence category.

(b) manual vehicles only.

* (c) automatic vehicles only.

ACCIDENTS

WHAT ACTION TO TAKE

Q. You have been involved in an accident where nobody has been injured but the vehicles are causing danger or obstruction to other road users. You should .....

Ans. (a) halt all other traffic until blame has been established.

* (b) mark the position of the vehicles and move them off the road.

(c) wait for the Gardai to arrive before moving the vehicles off the road.

Q. What should you do if you are involved in an accident which you think was not your fault?

Ans. (a) Carry on to the nearest Garda station and report it as soon as possible.

* (b) Stop immediately and exchange particulars with the other person involved.

(c) Carry on if you think there was no damage done to your vehicle.

Q. If you have been involved in a road accident, you must notify your insurance company .....

Ans. (a) only when renewing your policy.

* (b) as soon as possible.

(c) only if a person has been injured.

COLLISION - NO INJURY

Q. If you are involved in a collision where minor damage is caused to both vehicles, you must .....

Ans. * (a) stop your vehicle and exchange particulars with the driver of the other vehicle.
(b) not report it to your insurance company.
(c) not report it to the Gardai.

Q. You have been involved in an accident where damage to property only has occurred. You should .....

Ans. (a) report the incident to the Gardai within 10 days.
(b) report the incident to the Gardai within 24 hours.
* (c) it is not necessary to report the incident to the Gardai provided it is reported to the property owner.

COLLISION - PERSON INJURED

Q. Where a person has been injured in an accident, you should .....

Ans. (a) move the vehicles out of the way to avoid causing obstruction.
(b) move the victim to the nearest shelter.
* (c) where fitted, switch on hazard warning lights and summon help.

Q. You come on the scene of an accident where a person has been injured. Should you give the person anything to drink?

Ans. * (a) No.
(b) A cold drink should be given if possible.
(c) A non-alcoholic drink should be given if possible.

Q. You have been involved in an accident and a person is unconscious. You should .....

Ans. * (a) loosen any tight clothing at the neck, and keep the person warm with a blanket or overcoat.
(b) move the person to the nearest hospital.
(c) try to get the person to drink something.

Q. You have arrived at the scene of an accident and a person is bleeding heavily. You should .....

Ans. (a) keep the person warm and give him/her something to drink.
* (b) try to stop the bleeding by putting on a tight bandage.
(c) put the person lying flat on the ground and prevent him/her from moving.

Q. You have been involved in an accident and a person has been injured. Which of these is the most correct procedure?

Ans. * (a) Do not move the person unless there is a danger of fire or of being hit by passing vehicles.

(b) Carry the person to the side of the road.

(c) Have the person move various limbs to determine the extent of the injuries.

Q. A person has been injured in a road accident. Who should be called first?

Ans. (a) The person's relatives.

* (b) An ambulance and the Gardai.

(c) The injured person's solicitor.

Q. You have been involved in an accident and a person has been injured. You should firstly .....

Ans. * (a) report it to the Gardai and the local ambulance service.

(b) report it to the local motor taxation office.

(c) report it to your insurance company.

EXCHANGE OF INFORMATION

Q.   You have been involved in an accident with a
           visiting uninsured motorist where no injury
           has occurred. You should report it to .....

Ans. * (a)   the Motor Insurers Bureau of Ireland and
                 your own insurance company.
         (b)   the Department of Foreign Affairs.
         (c)   your local motor taxation office.

Q.   If you are involved in a collision with another
           vehicle where nobody is injured, what must
           you do?

Ans. * (a)   Exchange all relevant particulars with the
                 other driver.
         (b)   Give your name and address only.
         (c)   Report it to the Gardai.

Q.   You have been involved in an accident.
           What details must you give to a Garda?

Ans. * (a)   Any details requested.
         (b)   Your name and address and a description of
               how the accident occurred.
         (c)   Your solicitor's name and address and the
               details of your driving licence.

HAZARDOUS MATERIALS

Q.   You come on the scene of an accident
involving a vehicle carrying hazardous
materials. You should .....

Ans.   (a)   try to establish the nature of the hazardous
materials before raising the alarm.

(b)   try to move the vehicle to a safe place.

*   (c)   keep well clear and raise the alarm.

SAFETY FACTORS RELATING TO VEHICLE AND PERSONS CARRIED

CHILD PASSENGERS

Q.　What is the greatest danger in allowing children to stand in the space between the front seats of a vehicle?

Ans.　(a)　They could become ill.

*　(b)　They could be thrown forward if the brakes are applied suddenly.

(c)　They could be thrown backwards if the brakes are applied suddenly.

Q.　Should you allow children to stand with their heads up through an open sun-roof.

Ans.　(a)　Yes at speeds below 30 m.p.h..

(b)　Yes provided they wear eye protection.

*　(c)　No.

CARRYING OF PASSENGER

Q.　A category W provisional licence holder may carry a passenger on a tractor or works vehicle when .....

Ans.　(a)　the passenger has personal insurance cover.

(b)　the driver holds a full motorcycle licence.

*　(c)　there is proper passenger seating and the passenger holds a 'full' category W licence.

Q. Should young children or infants be left unattended in a vehicle?

Ans. (a) Yes, provided there is adequate ventilation.
(b) Yes, provided the vehicle is not parked on a hill.
* (c) No.

CHILDREN DRIVING

Q. When should children be allowed to drive a tractor?

Ans. * (a) Never.
(b) When it is off the public road.
(c) When it is being driven at slow speeds.

EFFECT OF IMPACT ON PASSENGERS

Q. What is the immediate effect of a head-on impact of two cars at speed?

Ans. * (a) All persons in the vehicles are thrown violently forward.
(b) The fuel systems in both vehicles shut down in order to prevent fire.
(c) Both vehicles' safety features will activate to prevent any injury to the occupants.

CARRYING A PASSENGER ON A MOTORCYCLE

Q. How would you maintain your balance on a motorcycle while carrying a passenger?

Ans. * (a) Instruct the passenger to sit astride the machine and to lean over on bends in the same direction as yourself.

(b) Negotiate bends at a higher speed than normal.

(c) Lean forward more than normal.

Q. You should maintain balance on the motorcycle when carrying a passenger by .....

Ans. (a) instructing the passenger to lean in the opposite direction to you on bends.

(b) ensuring that the passengers body weight is centred as much as possible over the rear wheel.

* (c) ensuring that the passenger sits astride the machine and leans in the same direction as you on bends.

Q. When carrying a passenger on a motorcycle, you should ensure that the passenger wears .....

Ans. * (a) a helmet with an adjustable visor.

(b) leather boots.

(c) rain protection clothing.

Q.   When should a passenger sit sideways on a motorcycle?

Ans. * (a)   Never.
              (b)   When the roads are wet.
              (c)   When strong side winds are blowing.

Q.   To ensure protection for your eyes when riding a motorcycle, you should .....

Ans. * (a)   wear a helmet with an adjustable visor.
              (b)   keep your head angled downwards.
              (c)   keep your eyes partially closed.

Q.   On what occasions may you drive a motorcycle in a public place without wearing a helmet?

Ans.   (a)   Inside the 30 m.p.h. speed limit areas.
              (b)   When travelling on minor roads at speeds below 30 m.p.h.
        *   (c)   Never.

SEVERE BRAKING

Q. **What danger can arise if you have to brake suddenly?**

Ans * (a) Both yourself and your passenger(s), if any, could be thrown forward.

(b) Your vehicle's braking system could lose brake fluid.

(c) Both yourself and your passenger(s), if any, could be thrown backwards.

SAFETY

Q. **What danger can arise with the power takeoff of a tractor?**

Ans. * (a) Clothing can get caught in it if it is not covered.

(b) It can cause the engine to increase speed rapidly.

(c) It can cause the battery to short-circuit.

LOAD CARRYING CAPACITY

Q. **What determines a vehicle's total load carrying capacity?**

Ans. (a) The size of the boot.

(b) The number of seats.

* (c) The vehicle manufacturer's specification.

Q.   **Are you allowed to carry more passengers in your car than there are seats available?**

Ans.   (a)   Yes, provided the passengers do not interfere with your visibility.

*   (b)   No.

(c)   Yes, provided you have appropriate insurance cover.

Q.   **You have been asked to drive a vehicle which you feel is overloaded. You should .....**

Ans.   (a)   drive at a slower speed than you normally would.

*   (b)   refuse to drive the vehicle.

(c)   advise the person who asked you that you will not be held responsible if an accident occurs.

Q.   **What defines the maximum allowed towing capacity of a drawing vehicle?**

Ans.   (a)   The strength of the hitch.

*   (b)   The manufacturer's specifications.

(c)   The size of the tyres on the vehicle.

LOAD DISTRIBUTION

Q.   **What effect would overloading a vehicle have on road-holding?**

Ans.   (a)   It would improve the stability of the vehicle provided the load was evenly distributed.

*   (b)   It could make the vehicle more difficult to control.

        (c)   It would not have any effect provided you drive slowly.

Q.   **What effect could overloading with passengers or goods have on a vehicle?**

Ans.   (a)   It could improve the vehicle's road-holding ability.

*   (b)   It could lessen the vehicle's road-holding ability.

        (c)   It would not have any effect provided you drive slowly.

Q.   **How could towing an overloaded trailer affect your vehicle?**

Ans.   (a)   It could improve the vehicle's fuel consumption.

        (b)   It could improve road holding on bends.

*   (c)   It could impair the vehicle's steering and braking.

Q. You are carrying some small packages in your vehicle. Which of these is the safest place to put them?

Ans. * (a) On the rear seat or on the floor.
     (b) On the rear window ledge.
     (c) On the front windscreen ledge.

Q. How could an unevenly distributed load affect your vehicle?

Ans. * (a) It could make the vehicle unstable while cornering or braking.
     (b) It could cause the clutch to slip while accelerating.
     (c) It could cause the gearbox to overheat.

POSITION WHEN CORNERING

Q. When cornering, a motorcyclist should .....

Ans. * (a) lean in the direction of the turn.
     (b) lean in the opposite direction to the turn.
     (c) remain in an upright position.

TRAILERS

Q. **What should you ensure when attaching a trailer to a vehicle?**

Ans.
    (a)   That the trailer springs are well greased.

    (b)   That the trailer has a spare wheel.

*   (c)   That any load in the trailer is evenly spread so that the hitch will not become detached.

Q. **Before un-hitching a trailer from a towing vehicle, you should firstly .....**

Ans.
    (a)   disconnect the electrical supply to the trailer lights and lower the jockey wheel.

*   (b)   apply the hand brake with a low gear engaged and switch off the ignition.

    (c)   lower the jockey wheel and then switch off the ignition.

Q. **When may you carry a passenger on a trailer drawbar?**

Ans. * (a)   Never.

    (b)   Anytime.

    (c)   When towing a trailer off-road.

VEHICLE HANDLING

Q. A tractor is most likely to overturn when .....

Ans.
    (a)   speeding on the flat.
  * (b)   speeding downhill.
    (c)   speeding uphill.

Q. What should you do to avoid possible roll-over on entering a roundabout when driving a tractor with a trailer?

Ans. * (a)   Reduce speed.
    (b)   Increase speed.
    (c)   Engage the parking brake.

Q. Jack-knifing is .....

Ans.
    (a)   when the trailer is too heavy to be drawn by the tractor.
  * (b)   when the trailer is trying to travel faster than the drawing tractor.
    (c)   when the jack is not strong enough to lift an axle.

Q. When might jack-knifing occur?

Ans.
    (a)   Travelling sideways across a slope.
    (b)   Travelling uphill.
  * (c)   When trying to reduce speed sharply while travelling downhill.

Q.   You wish to turn right when driving a tractor with a wide load which is blocking your view to the rear. What should you do?

Ans.   (a)   Dismount and check for following traffic before turning.

(b)   Complete the turn if there is no traffic coming towards you.

* (c)   Have a person advise you of traffic from behind while you check for oncoming traffic.

TECHNICAL MATTERS, WITH A BEARING ON ROAD SAFETY

HEADLIGHTS

Q.   **Why is it important to ensure that your vehicle's headlights are correctly focused?**

Ans.   (a)   To reduce battery consumption.
       (b)   To enable you to drive faster in the dark.
  * (c)   To enable you to see properly.

Q.   **If your vehicle's headlights were incorrectly aimed .....**

Ans.   (a)   the bulbs would have to be replaced frequently.
  * (b)   the headlight beams would not shine light correctly on the road ahead.
       (c)   a warning light would appear on the dash.

Q.   **Incorrectly focused headlights could .....**

Ans.   *   (a)   dazzle oncoming drivers.
       (b)   increase battery consumption.
       (c)   cause a fire.

Q.   In general, how frequently should your
        vehicle's lights be checked?

Ans.   (a)   Monthly.
         (b)   Annually.
      * (c)   Weekly.

Q.   What effect can a broken lens have on a
        headlight.

Ans.   * (a)   It can reduce and distort the beam.
         (b)   It can increase the brightness of the beam.
         (c)   It can cause the bulb to overheat.

SIDELIGHTS

Q.   You should drive with side-lights on when .....

Ans.   * (a)   the daylight is fading.
         (b)   driving in an unlit area at night.
         (c)   driving at more than 50 m.p.h.

Q.   How would you know if a side-lamp bulb had
        failed?

Ans.   (a)   None of the lights would operate when
                 switched on.
         (b)   A warning buzzer would sound when the
                 sidelights are switched on.
      * (c)   By checking the sidelights when switched on.

BRAKE LIGHTS

Q.   How would you know if a brake-light bulb was not working?

Ans.   (a)   The brake pedal would feel 'soft'.

          (b)   The remaining brake light would be brighter than normal.

    *   (c)   Press the brake pedal while another person checks the lights from behind.

Q.   You are changing down through the gears in order to reduce speed. How does this affect your brake-lights?

Ans. * (a)   It has no effect on them.

          (b)   It causes them to light up.

          (c)   It causes them to flash briefly.

WARNING LIGHTS

Q.   If a warning light starts flashing on the dashboard of your vehicle, you should .....

Ans. * (a)   stop and check the problem.

          (b)   carry on and check the problem later.

          (c)   continue for a distance to see if the light will go out.

Q. If a red warning light on the dash-board lights up as you drive along, you should .....

Ans.   (a)   drive to the nearest garage and have it checked.
        (b)   continue on and see if it will go out.
  * (c)   stop and investigate the cause.

Q. What effect do the hazard warning lights on your vehicle have on the brake-lights?

Ans. * (a)   No effect.
        (b)   It causes them to flash repeatedly.
        (c)   It causes the left and right brake-lights to flash alternately.

Q. When should you use your hazard warning lights?

Ans.   (a)   When about to overtake.
        (b)   When about to pull in and stop.
  * (c)   When causing an unavoidable obstruction.

Q. You should use your vehicle's hazard warning lights when .....

Ans.   (a)   you are double-parking.
  * (b)   you have broken down.
        (c)   your brake-lights are not working.

Q.   **What lighting should be on a car-trailer?**

Ans.   (a)   None.

           (b)   Indicators and rear number plate light.

    *   (c)   Indicators, brake-lights, rear number plate light, red reflectors, and rear tail lights.

Q.   **What lighting should be on a tractor trailer during lighting up hours?**

Ans.   (a)   None.

           (b)   Indicators and rear number plate light.

    *   (c)   Indicators, brake-lights, rear number plate light, red reflectors, and rear tail light.

REFLECTORS

Q.   **What is the purpose of your vehicle's reflectors?**

Ans.   (a)   They are a substitute in case of brake-light failure.

           (b)   They warn the driver behind to switch to dipped headlights.

    *   (c)   They reflect light at night in order to make other road users aware of your vehicle.

INDICATORS

Q. **A rapid clicking noise when you operate the indicator switch suggests that .....**

Ans * (a) an indicator bulb has blown.

(b) the front and rear indicators are not working in tandem.

(c) the hazard warning lights are on.

BRAKES

Q. **What does A.B.S. do?**

Ans. (a) It displays the name of the radio station playing on the car radio.

(b) It clears condensation from the windows.

* (c) It prevents the wheels from locking under harsh braking conditions.

Q. **Generally, the handbrake operates on .....**

Ans. (a) the front wheels.

* (b) the rear wheels.

(c) all the wheels.

Q. **If the brake pedal feels 'soft' or 'slack' when applied, what could it mean?**

Ans. (a) Worn brake pads.

(b) Worn handbrake cable.

* (c) Low brake fluid level, or alternatively worn cable in the motorcycle.

Q.   If the brake fluid is low, the brakes would .....

Ans.   (a)   be unusually sharp.
       (b)   take longer than usual to release.
    * (c)   feel spongy and soft.

Q.   You hear a scraping noise when the footbrake is applied. What is the likely cause?

Ans.   (a)   There is too much oil on the brakes.
    * (b)   The brake linings are worn.
       (c)   There is not enough oil on the brakes.

Q.   How would you know that there is a problem in the condition of your vehicle's brakes?

Ans.   (a)   The vehicle's suspension would be affected.
       (b)   The vehicle would be sluggish when moving off.
    * (c)   The vehicle's stopping ability would be affected.

Q.   In general, trailers above what gross vehicle weight must have brakes fitted?

Ans.   (a)   500 kg.
    * (b)   750 kg.
       (c)   1,000 kg.

AUTOMATIC TRANSMISSION

Q.   **What is the recommended method of driving a vehicle with automatic transmission?**

Ans.   *   (a)   Operate the accelerator and brake with the right foot.

           (b)   Operate the accelerator and brake with the left foot.

           (c)   Operate the accelerator with the right foot and the brake with the left foot.

Q.   **If driving a vehicle with automatic transmission, you should be aware that .....**

Ans.   *   (a)   engine braking power is reduced.

           (b)   wheel-spin occurs more often.

           (c)   the gearbox may overheat while being driven in low gear.

Q.   **What effect does automatic transmission have on an engine's braking power?**

Ans.   *   (a)   It reduces it.

           (b)   It increases it.

           (c)   It transfers the braking power to all the wheels.

VEHICLE CONDITION (ENGINE)

Q. **When driving along you notice that your engine power is lower than normal. You should .....**

Ans.   (a)   switch to a different fuel.

        (b)   adjust the fuel mixture control screw.

   * (c)   have the vehicle checked by a competent mechanic as soon as possible.

FUEL

Q. **When driving a diesel engined vehicle in cold weather, you should ensure that .....**

Ans. * (a)   the fuel is treated with an anti-waxing agent.

        (b)   the fuel filter is drained.

        (c)   the fuel level in the tank does not drop below quarter full.

BODY CONDITION

Q. **If you notice that parts of your vehicle's body are affected by rust, you should .....**

Ans.   (a)   have paint sprayed over it of the same colour.

        (b)   have it sandpapered and keep the affected area dry.

   * (c)   have it assessed and treated if necessary by a competent repair shop.

BATTERY

Q.   **What effect would a weakly charged battery have on your vehicle's driving performance?**

Ans. * (a)   It would have no effect.

         (b)   The fuel would burn less efficiently.

         (c)   Uphill acceleration would be reduced.

SHOCK ABSORBERS/SUSPENSION

Q.   **Which of the following effects could a worn shock absorber have on a vehicle?**

Ans.   (a)   It could increase fuel consumption.

       * (b)   It could cause the vehicle to 'bounce' in an unstable manner.

         (c)   It could lessen braking power.

MIRRORS

Q.   **When driving, your mirror(s) should reflect .....**

Ans. * (a)   the area behind and each side to the rear of your vehicle.

         (b)   the passenger area of the vehicle.

         (c)   the area behind and to each side of the vehicle.

Q. Your vehicle's wing mirror(s) should .....

Ans.
    (a)   show the side(s) of the vehicle only.
    (b)   not show the side(s) of the vehicle.
  * (c)   show the side(s) of the vehicle and also the road to the side(s) and to the rear of the vehicle.

Q. What effect could wet weather have on your vehicle's exterior mirrors?

Ans.
    (a)   It could keep them clean.
  * (b)   It could make the image shown in them less clear.
    (c)   It could cause a short circuit in electrically heated mirrors.

Q. When must a tractor or works vehicle be fitted with a rear-view mirror?

Ans.
    (a)   It is not required.
  * (b)   Always.
    (c)   Only when towing a trailer.

EXHAUST

Q. Blue smoke coming from your vehicle's exhaust suggests that .,....

Ans.
    (a)   the catalytic converter is worn out.
  * (b)   the engine is burning oil.
    (c)   the choke is engaged.

Q.   **What would be the effect of a worn exhaust?**

Ans. * (a)   The filtering of fumes would be reduced and engine noise would be louder.

         (b)   The engine would overheat.

         (c)   Gear-changing would be more difficult.

Q.   **How could a faulty exhaust affect your vehicle?**

Ans.   (a)   It could lessen engine noise.

         (b)   It could improve fuel consumption.

    * (c)   It could increase the noise and pollution levels of the vehicle.

Q.   **What is the purpose of a catalytic converter?**

Ans.   (a)   It allows the engine to quickly reach its normal operating temperature.

         (b)   It increases engine power.

    * (c)   It filters exhaust gases thereby minimising air pollution.

TYRES

Q.   **What is the minimum legal tread depth for tyres on cars?**

Ans.   (a)   0.8 millimetres.

         (b)   1.0 millimetres.

    * (c)   1.6 millimetres.

Q. What is the minimum legal tyre tread depth for motorcycles?

Ans.
    (a)   3 millimetres.
    (b)   2 millimetres.
* (c)   I millimetre.

Q. What is the minimum tread depth required for tractor tyres?

Ans.
    (a)   I mm.
    (b)   0.8 mm.
* (c)   1.6 mm.

Q. What effect would low tyre pressure have on a vehicle?

Ans.
    (a)   Engine noise would increase.
    (b)   The brakes could overheat.
* (c)   Braking and cornering of the vehicle would be affected.

Q. You notice that one of your front tyres is worn. You should .....

Ans.
    (a)   reduce speed on wet roads.
    (b)   fit it on one of the rear wheels.
* (c)   have it replaced.

Q.   **What effect could hitting or mounting the kerb have on your vehicle's tyres?**

Ans.   (a)   It could allow air to escape from them.

      *   (b)   It could put the steering alignment out of line.

            (c)   It could put them off balance.

Q.   **A worn tread along the edge of a tyre suggests that .....**

Ans.   (a)   the air pressure is low.

            (b)   the air pressure is high.

      *   (c)   the steering alignment may be faulty.

Q.   **What effect would under-inflated tyres have on your vehicle's engine transmission?**

Ans.   (a)   They would make it more difficult to change gears.

            (b)   They would cause the clutch to overheat.

      *   (c)   They would have no effect on it.

Q.   **In general, how frequently should you check the tyre pressures on your vehicle?**

Ans.   *   (a)   Weekly.

            (b)   Monthly.

            (c)   Annually.

Q. When should both cross-ply and radial tyres be fitted to a vehicle?

Ans.
    (a)   When heavy loads are being carried.
    (b)   In icy or slippery road conditions.
  * (c)   Never.

Q. Before undertaking a long journey you should .....

Ans.
    (a)   reduce the air pressure in your tyres.
    (b)   increase the air pressure in your tyres.
  * (c)   check that your tyres have their normal air pressure.

Q. Is it advisable to put extra air pressure into the tyres when about to undertake a long journey?

Ans * (a)   No.
    (b)   Yes.
    (c)   Only if high speeds are anticipated.

Q. How would you detect a problem in the condition of a tyre?

Ans. * (a)   By a visual inspection, and checking the air pressure.
    (b)   By looking for a coloured wear indicator.
    (c)   By checking if the vehicle pulls to one side when the brakes are applied.

Q. **What effects would under inflated tyres have on a vehicle?**

Ans.   (a)   Improved braking and steering.
    * (b)   Impaired braking and steering.
       (c)   Improved fuel economy and braking.

Q. **What effect would coasting have on your vehicles tyres?**

Ans. * (a)   No effect.
       (b)   It would cause them to lose air pressure.
       (c)   It would increase the rate of wear on them.

Q. **To secure the vehicle when changing a wheel, you should .....**

Ans.   (a)   point the front wheels towards the kerb.
       (b)   ensure that the gear lever is in neutral.
   * (c)   ensure that the vehicle cannot roll when jacked up.

CLUTCH

Q. **Resting your foot on the clutch pedal .....**

Ans.   (a)   facilitates quicker gear changes.
   * (b)   wears out the clutch quicker.
       (c)   allows downhill speeds to be controlled more effectively.

Q. When driving along, where should you normally rest your left foot?

Ans. * (a) On the floor or footrest.
(b) On the clutch pedal.
(c) Under the brake pedal.

STEERING

Q. A continuous vibration in the steering wheel while driving could indicate that .....

Ans. * (a) the wheel balance is uneven.
(b) the shock absorbers are worn.
(c) weight distribution is uneven.

SEAT

Q. An incorrectly adjusted driver's seat could .....

Ans. * (a) cause a delay in the driver operating a control.
(b) enable the driver to relax more on a long journey.
(c) afford the driver a better view in the rear-view mirror.

WIPERS

Q.   **You are driving in the rain and your wiper blades are worn. You should .....**

Ans.   (a)   stop and wipe the windscreen with newspaper.

   (b)   use the windscreen washer system all the time while it rains.

*   (c)   drive slowly to the nearest garage and have the blades replaced.

Q.   **If the wipers are frozen to the windscreen, you should .....**

Ans.   (a)   switch the wipers to high speed to free them.

*   (b)   defrost the windscreen before switching on the wipers.

   (c)   pull the wipers free before switching them on.

Q.   **When a wiper blade fails to clear the windscreen satisfactorily, you should .....**

Ans.   (a)   apply a light film of oil to the blade.

   (b)   bend the wiper arm.

*   (c)   have the blade replaced as soon as possible.

Q. **What problem is indicated when wipers suddenly cease to function?**

Ans. (a) The windscreen washer reservoir is dry.
(b) The alternator is faulty.
* (c) A fuse has blown.

WINDSCREEN

Q. **A laminated windscreen .....**

Ans. * (a) is designed not to shatter into large fragments when struck by an object.
(b) is glass which has the registration number of the vehicle etched on to it.
(c) shatters into large fragments when struck by an object.

ENVIRONMENTAL MATTERS

FUEL CONSUMPTION

Q.   **How would harsh acceleration affect fuel consumption?**

Ans.   (a)   There would be no effect provided the engine is properly tuned.

* (b)   Fuel consumption would improve.

* (c)   Fuel consumption would increase.

Q.   **To achieve maximum fuel efficiency from your vehicle's engine, you should .....**

Ans.   (a)   drive with the choke out.

(b)   accelerate rapidly up through the gears.

* (c)   use gentle acceleration and braking.

Q   **Continuous high speed driving would .....**

Ans. *   (a)   increase fuel consumption.

(b)   reduce fuel consumption.

(c)   increase fuel consumption only in wet weather.

Q. To ensure better fuel efficiency from your vehicle, you should .....

Ans. (a) drive at higher speed in order to reduce the time spent on the road.

* (b) ensure that the vehicle is regularly serviced.

(c) ensure that heavier items are carried at the rear of the vehicle.

Q. Fuel efficiency is improved by .....

Ans. (a) accelerating hard up through the gears to reach the desired speed as quickly as possible.

(b) driving the vehicle in a lower gear for as long as possible.

* (c) using gentle acceleration and making gear changes as recommended by the manufacturer's specifications.

SMOKE

Q. A cloud of blue smoke on acceleration would suggest that .....

Ans. (a) the brakes are locked on.

(b) the wrong type of fuel is being used.

* (c) the engine needs to be serviced.

Q.   To avoid excessive exhaust pollution from your vehicle, you should .....

Ans.   (a)   drive at a higher speed in order to reduce the time spent on the road.

        (b)   use a fuel additive to increase the fuel octane rating.

    * (c)   change your vehicle's air filters regularly.

Q.   How regularly should your vehicle's engine be serviced?

Ans.   (a)   Every 20,000 miles.

        (b)   Every year.

    * (c)   In line with the manufacturer's specification.

Q.   If you take the exhaust off your motorcycle .....

Ans.   (a)   the engine would overheat.

        (b)   the engine oil would be contaminated.

    * (c)   the engine noise and smoke pollution would increase.

NOISE

Q.   What type of noise might fast cornering induce?

Ans. * (a)   Tyre squeal.

        (b)   Brake squeal.

        (c)   Exhaust backfire.

Q. **What effect does a worn exhaust have on a vehicle?**

Ans. (a) It causes oil to leak on to the road.
(b) It causes the water coolant to leak from the engine.
* (c) It causes noise and smoke pollution levels to increase.

HORN

Q. **Are you allowed to sound the horn while driving in a built-up area at night?**

Ans. (a) Yes but only between 11.30 p.m. and 7 a.m..
(b) No.
* (c) Yes but only in an emergency between 11.30 p.m. and 7.00 a.m..

Q. **Are you allowed to use a musical horn on your vehicle?**

Ans. * (a) No.
(b) Yes.
(c) Yes, but only during daylight hours.

GETTING OUT FROM, OR OFF, THE VEHICLE

Q.   You have just stopped and wish to get out of your vehicle. Which of the following is the most correct action for you to take?

Ans.   *   (a)   Check your side mirror and look behind before opening the door.

(b)   Check your inside mirror before opening the door.

(c)   Open the door part way and then look behind.

Q.   What should you do to secure the vehicle before getting out of it?

Ans.   (a)   Make sure it is fully unloaded.

*   (b)   Engage a low gear, apply the parking brake and switch off the ignition.

(c)   Make sure all valuables are out of sight and that the steering lock is engaged.

Q.   What precautions should you take when getting out of your vehicle?

Ans.   (a)   Open the door and try to get out as speedily as possible.

(b)   Ensure the gear lever is in neutral.

*   (c)   Check all around for oncoming traffic/pedestrians before opening the door.

Q. **What precautions should you take before getting out of the vehicle?**

Ans.   (a)   Leave the engine running.

        (b)   Switch off the engine and make sure the gear is in neutral.

    *   (c)   Switch off the engine, apply the hand brake and engage a low gear.

Q. **You are driving on a busy road and you wish to stop to allow passengers out of your vehicle. You should .....**

Ans.   (a)   stop and allow them to get out from whichever side of the vehicle they are sitting on.

    *   (b)   stop and allow them to get out on the side nearest the kerb.

        (c)   stop and ask them to get out as quickly as possible.

Q. **What precautions should you take on getting off a motorcycle?**

Ans.   (a)   First park the machine on its stand and then switch off the ignition and remove the key.

        (b)   Lean the machine against a wall or support.

    *   (c)   First switch off the ignition, park the machine on its stand and remove the key.

Q.   **When a passenger is getting off your motorcycle, you should ensure that .....**

Ans.   (a)   the motorcycle is always resting on its stand.

*   (b)   the motorcycle is always stopped in a safe place.

(c)   the passenger gets off from the right-hand side of the motorcycle.

VEHICLE SAFETY EQUIPMENT

SEAT-BELTS

Q.   **What cars are required to have rear seat-belts fitted?**

Ans. * (a)   Cars first registered after 1st January, 1992.
          (b)   Only cars first registered prior to 1st January 1992.
          (c)   All cars.

Q.   **All car occupants must normally wear seat-belts where they are fitted .....**

Ans.   (a)   on long journeys only.
            (b)   except in built-up areas.
       *   (c)   at all times.

Q.   **The purpose of a seat-belt is .....**

Ans. * (a)   to prevent the wearer from being thrown forward in the event of an accident.
          (b)   to keep the seat upright in the event of an accident.
          (c)   to prevent the seat from moving forward when the brakes are applied.

Q.　　When starting off in your car, you should .....

Ans.　*　(a)　put on your seat-belt before you move off.
　　　　(b)　put on your seat-belt not later than the time you engage top gear.
　　　　(c)　put on your seat-belt once you are outside the 30 m.p.h. speed limit zone.

Q.　　When carrying passengers who are aged 17 years or more the responsibility for wearing a seat-belt is .....

Ans.　　(a)　on the driver.
　　*　(b)　on the passengers.
　　　　(c)　on both the driver and the passengers.

CHILDREN'S SAFETY SEATS

Q.　　Who is responsible for ensuring that a child wears a safety-belt in a vehicle?

Ans.　　(a)　The child.
　　*　(b)　The driver.
　　　　(c)　The child's parent(s).

Q.　　When carrying passengers who are under 17 years of age, who is responsible for ensuring that they are wearing seat-belts?

Ans.　*　(a)　The driver.
　　　　(b)　The passengers themselves.
　　　　(c)　The passengers' parents.

Q. In general, how should infants be secured in a vehicle?

Ans.
    (a)   They should always be carried on an adults lap.

    (b)   They should always be placed in the front passenger seat.

* (c)   They should always be secured in a child safety seat or wear a seat-belt.

Q. Should infants who are not secured in a child safety seat be carried in the front passenger seat?

    (a)   Yes.

    (b)   Yes if held by an adult.

* (c)   No.

Q. How should a child safety seat be secured in a vehicle?

Ans.
    (a)   It should be placed on a normal passenger seat.

* (b)   It should be secured with the existing seat belts, or with additional straps.

    (c)   It should be left unsecured.

Q. **What should you do when driving a vehicle which is carrying young children?**

Ans. (a) Turn on the radio to keep them entertained.

(b) Exchange them regularly between the front and rear seats so that they do not become bored.

* (c) Make sure each child is wearing a seat-belt or using an appropriate restraint system.

SIDE IMPACT PROTECTION BARS

Q. **What is the purpose of side impact protection bars?**

Ans. (a) To make sure that the vehicle cannot be overturned when hit from the side.

(b) To enhance the vehicle's braking system.

* (c) To protect the occupants when the vehicle is hit from the side.

CHAPTER 2

Part I

CATEGORIES C and D

NECESSARY DOCUMENTS

Q.   **What vehicles are required to have a Certificate of Roadworthiness issued each year?**

Ans. * (a)   Vehicles with more than 8 passenger seats, and goods vehicles with a gross vehicle weight over 3,500 kg.

          (b)   Goods vehicles with a gross vehicle weight over 10,000 kg.

          (c)   Only goods vehicles with a gross vehicle weight over 3,500 kg.

Q.   **How frequently must your vehicle be submitted for a certificate of roadworthiness test?**

Ans. * (a)   Annually.

          (b)   Every 2 years.

          (c)   Every 3 years.

Q. What provisionally licensed drivers in Categories C, C1, D and D1 are not required to be accompanied by the holder of a full licence?

Ans. * (a) None.
(b) Drivers aged 21 years or more.
(c) Holders of 2nd provisional licences only.

DRIVING HOURS, AND REST PERIODS

Q. The maximum permitted number of driving hours without taking a break is .....

Ans. (a) 3 hours.
* (b) 4.5 hours.
(c) 5 hours.

Q. The maximum number of hours you may drive in a given week is .....

Ans. * (a) 56 hours.
(b) 46 hours.
(c) 50 hours.

Q. The maximum permitted number of driving hours in a fortnight is .....

Ans. (a) 70 hours.
(b) 80 hours.
* (c) 90 hours.

Q.   The minimum break time which should be taken for each break during or following a driving period is .....

Ans. * (a)   15 minutes.
            (b)   30 minutes.
            (c)   45 minutes.

Q.   The minimum break time which must be taken following a 4.5 hour driving period is .....

Ans.   (a)   30 mins.
        *   (b)   45 mins.
            (c)   1 hour.

Q.   You have driven for 56 hours in the first week of a two-week period. The maximum number of hours you may drive in the second week is .....

Ans.   (a)   44 hours.
        *   (b)   34 hours.
            (c)   54 hours.

Q.   Who is responsible for ensuring that a tachograph sheet is properly completed and inserted into the tachograph?

Ans.   (a)   The owner of the vehicle.
            (b)   The hire company.
        *   (c)   The driver.

Q. **What information is recorded on a tachograph sheet?**

Ans.   (a)   Distance covered and average fuel consumption.

       (b)   Fuel consumption and vehicle speed.

     *   (c)   Driving time, vehicle speed and distance covered.

Q. **Used tachograph sheets must be retained for .....**

Ans.   (a)   the 7 days on which you drove.

       (b)   the 14 days on which you drove.

     *   (c)   the current week and the last day of the previous week on which you drove.

Q. **When must a new tachograph sheet be placed in a tachograph?**

Ans. *   (a)   At the start of each working day.

       (b)   At 12 midnight on each working day.

       (c)   Every 12 hours of each working day.

Q. **What time and day denote the beginning of a week for tachograph purposes?**

Ans.   (a)   0600 hours on Monday.

       (b)   0800 hours on Monday.

     *   (c)   00.00 hours on Monday.

Q. What is the danger in not complying with break period requirements?

Ans. * (a) The driver could become tired while driving.

(b) The tachograph could disconnect.

(c) The tachograph could record incorrect times.

Q. A driver's rest period may be taken in a parked vehicle if .....

Ans. * (a) it is fitted with a bunk.

(b) there are no passengers on board.

(c) the windows of the vehicle are left open.

VEHICLE WEIGHTS AND DIMENSIONS.

Q. The maximum permitted rear-load overhang which does not require a red flag or marker is .....

Ans. * (a) I metre.

(b) 2 metres.

(c) 3 metres.

Q. The maximum permitted rear-load overhang with a red flag is .....

Ans. (a) I metre.

(b) 2 metres.

* (c) 3 metres.

Q.   The maximum permitted side-load overhang
is .....

Ans.   * (a)   1 foot.
(b)   2 feet.
(c)   3 feet.

Q.   What does design gross vehicle weight mean?

Ans.   * (a)   Vehicle weight plus maximum load weight
which it is designed to carry.
(b)   The maximum load weight less the vehicle
weight.
(c)   The maximum weight for the licence
category.

BRAKING SYSTEMS

Q.   Freezing weather could cause your air brakes
to .....

Ans.   (a)   be faster to grip on the brake drums.
(b)   be slower to grip on the brake drums.
* (c)   freeze up if the moisture has not been
drained from the air-tanks.

Q. **What could cause your foot-brake to become less effective?**

Ans. (a) Continuous starting and stopping of the vehicle.

(b) The air system overheating due to warm weather.

* (c) Continuous use of the foot-brake on a long descent.

Q. **What could cause brake-fade?**

Ans. (a) Low air or low fluid pressure in the brake system.

(b) An incorrectly fitted tyre.

* (c) Continuous use of the foot-brake on a long descent.

Q. **Brake-fade is .....**

Ans. (a) low brake fluid.

(b) worn brake-drums.

* (c) reduced braking power due to over-heating.

Q. **An 'exhaust brake' .....**

Ans. (a) regulates the density of the exhaust fumes.

* (b) increases the braking ability of the engine.

(c) applies exhaust gas to the brakes to blow the dust off them.

Q. An inefficient compressor could affect your vehicle's brakes by .....

Ans. (a) making them unusually sharp.
   * (b) delivering a reduced supply of air to the airtanks.
     (c) causing the air-lines to collapse.

Q. A speed governor .....

Ans. (a) maintains the vehicle at a constant speed.
     (b) prevents the engine from over-revving.
   * (c) prevents the vehicle from exceeding a pre-set speed.

Q. The vehicle's speed can be controlled without using the foot-brake by .....

Ans. (a) applying the diff-lock.
   * (b) engaging the retarder.
     (c) pressing the clutch pedal.

Q. Given similar road conditions and vehicle speeds, what braking distances will a truck or bus/minibus need compared to a car?

Ans. * (a) Longer distances.
     (b) Shorter distances.
     (c) The same.

TECHNICAL MATTERS, WITH A BEARING ON ROAD SAFETY

Q.   **A load sensing valve .....**

Ans.   (a)   warns the driver when a gear-shift is required.

       (b)   warns the driver when the vehicle is overloaded.

     * (c)   adjusts the air pressure which is applied at the wheels.

Q.   **'Road-friendly' suspension .....**

Ans. * (a)   reduces the impact of a vehicle's weight on the road.

       (b)   increases the impact of a vehicle's weight on the road.

       (c)   allows vehicles to exceed the weight restrictions on bridges.

Q.   **A defective power assisted steering system would .....**

Ans.   (a)   make the steering seem light and easy to turn.

     * (b)   make the steering seem heavy and stiff to turn.

       (c)   cause the front tyres to lose pressure.

Q. **Where would you first look to investigate a problem in the power steering?**

Ans. * (a) In the hydraulic fluid reservoir.
(b) In the ignition system.
(c) In the compressed air system.

Q. **How might 'coasting' affect your brakes?**

Ans. (a) It would have no effect.
* (b) It would reduce the air supply available for use by the brakes.
(c) It would increase the air supply available for use by the brakes.

Q. **How would you know if a brake-light was defective?**

Ans. * (a) Have a person stand at the rear of the vehicle while you press the brake pedal.
(b) A warning light would appear on the dash.
(c) A clicking noise would be heard when the brakes are applied.

Q. **A diff-lock .....**

Ans. (a) improves the security of the vehicle by ensuring that the wheels can not be stolen.
(b) holds the selected gear to improve traction on steep slopes.
* (c) equalises traction at each drive wheel to improve grip in mud or snow.

Q.   What effect could wet weather have on your vehicle's exterior mirrors?

Ans.   (a)   It could keep them clean.
   * (b)   It could distort the image shown in them.
    (c)   It could cause a short circuit in electrically heated mirrors.

Q.   Frozen air-lines on your vehicle's braking system would .....

Ans.   (a)   cause a delay operating the brakes.
   * (b)   prevent pressurised air from operating the brakes.
    (c)   cause the wheel-rims to crack.

Q.   When driving, your mirror(s) should reflect .....

Ans.   * (a)   the area to each side and behind your vehicle.
    (b)   the passenger area of the vehicle.
    (c)   the area behind the vehicle.

AIR TURBULENCE

Q.   Air turbulence caused by the fast speed of a high sided vehicle could have most effect on .....

Ans.   * (a)   pedestrians walking at the side of the road.
    (b)   buses.
    (c)   stationary trucks.

Q. **What effect could your vehicle's slipstream have when overtaking a motorcyclist?**

Ans. * (a)   The motorcyclist could be blown off course.
(b)   The motorcyclist could drive at a faster speed.
(c)   The motorcyclist could be deafened by the wind noise.

Q. **What effect could your vehicle's slipstream have on a cyslist?**

Ans. * (a)   It could affect the cyclist's stability.
(b)   It would have no effect provided you keep within the speed limit.
(c)   It could draw the cyclist in towards your vehicle.

Q. **Dust or debris displaced from the road by your vehicle could .....**

Ans. (a)   block the exhaust.
(b)   cause the brake's air-lines to collapse.
* (c)   discomfort pedestrians or cyclists and affect their visibility.

Q. What should you be aware of when passing pedestrians at speed?

Ans. * (a) They could be affected by your vehicle's slipstream.

(b) They will hear the noise of your vehicle and keep in.

(c) The wing mirrors on your vehicle are always high enough to avoid hitting them.

WEATHER RELATED MATTERS

Q. What weather conditions could affect the air supply to your vehicle's brakes?

Ans. * (a) Freezing weather.

(b) Hot weather.

(c) Wet weather.

Q. Your vehicle exceeds 20 feet in length. What lights must it show when parked at night on a public road?

Ans. * (a) Side-lamps front and rear and number plate lighting.

(b) No lights are required provided it is parked on the left-hand side of the road.

(c) No lights are required.

Q. When you intend to start out on a long journey in bad weather conditions, you should .....

Ans.
    (a)   enquire as to the weather and road conditions at your destination.

  * (b)   check the weather forecast for information about road and weather conditions relating to your journey.

    (c)   reduce tyre pressures to ensure better grip on the roads.

Q. When driving a diesel engined vehicle in cold weather, you should ensure that .....

Ans. * (a)   the fuel is treated with an anti-waxing agent.

    (b)   the fuel filter is drained.

    (c)   the fuel level in the tank does not drop below quarter full.

Q. When driving in heavy rain, you should .....

Ans.
    (a)   engage the diff-lock mechanism.

    (b)   switch your windscreen wipers onto high speed and drive at normal speed.

  * (c)   switch your windscreen wipers onto high speed and decrease the speed of your vehicle to allow for reduced visibility.

Q. How should a descent be negotiated in snow or frosty weather?

Ans. (a) Engage a higher gear than normal in order to avoid wheelspin.

(b) Always keep close to the left and use short sharp brake applications to keep the speed down.

* (c) Use a retarder, if fitted, or lower gear, and use gentle brake applications to keep the speed down.

Q. What precautions would you take to avoid mud or spray from other vehicles when overtaking?

Ans. (a) Increase speed in order to reduce the time spent in the danger area.

(b) Drive close to the other vehicle in order to make use of its slipstream.

* (c) Use your vehicle's wipers and windscreen washer system.

Q When you are proposing to overtake a large vehicle that is throwing up spray, you should .....

Ans. (a) move close to the vehicle.

* (b) move out earlier than normal and give extra clearance.

(c) overtake in an exaggerated loop.

Q. **What effect could strong winds have on a high-sided vehicle?**

Ans. * (a) It could make it more liable to turn over.
(b) It could improve stability.
(c) It could affect the braking and suspension mechanisms.

Q. **Which of the following is the most stable in windy conditions?**

Ans. (a) A high-sided vehicle without a load.
(b) A high-sided vehicle with an uneven load.
* (c) A fully loaded high-sided vehicle.

Q. **What should you avoid when driving a high-sided vehicle in strong winds?**

Ans. (a) Underground roads.
(b) Steep hills.
* (c) Suspension bridges.

DRIVING LARGE OR HIGH-SIDED VEHICLES

Q. **What effect could strong winds have on a light high-sided vehicle?**

Ans. * (a) They could lessen stability.
(b) They could improve stability.
(c) They could reduce loading capacity.

Q.   What precaution should you take when driving around a roundabout to avoid roll-over?

Ans.   *   (a)   Reduce speed.
            (b)   Increase speed.
            (c)   Brake sharply.

Q.   What gear would you normally engage before descending a steep hill?

Ans.   (a)   One gear higher than would be used to climb it.
        *   (b)   One gear lower than would be used to climb it.
            (c)   The same gear as would be used to climb it.

Q.   When driving a vehicle with a low body over a steep hump-backed bridge, you should be aware of .....

Ans.   *   (a)   ground clearance.
            (b)   tyre pressures.
            (c)   tail-swing.

Q.   What aspects of your vehicle should be borne in mind when planning a route?

Ans.   *   (a)   The length, width and height of the vehicle.
            (b)   The type of transmission on the vehicle.
            (c)   The length and width of the vehicle.

Q. When entering a loading bay or refuelling depot you should be aware of .....

Ans.   (a)   the height of the vehicle.

         (b)   the width of the vehicle.

  *   (c)   the height and width of the vehicle.

Q. A driver of a vehicle with a high centre of gravity should be aware that .....

Ans. *   (a)   the vehicle is more likely to roll over on a bend.

         (b)   the vehicle is more stable than a similar vehicle with a low centre of gravity.

         (c)   fuel consumption is higher than a vehicle with a low centre of gravity.

Q. How does a short-wheelbase vehicle's handling differ from that of a long-wheelbase vehicle?

Ans.   (a)   It is more stable at high speed.

  *   (b)   It is less stable at high speed.

         (c)   There is no difference.

Q. **Why would you sometimes move to the right before making a left hand turn?**

Ans. * (a) In order to ensure that the inside rear wheels clear the corner.
(b) In order to prevent following traffic from overtaking in a dangerous manner.
(c) In order to allow following drivers to see what you are doing.

RESTRICTED VISION

Q. **What effect can sunlight have on grimy windows?**

Ans. (a) It can enhance visibility.
* (b) It can create a mirror effect and reduce visibility.
(c) It can eliminate a heavy build-up of condensation on the windows.

Q. **What action would you take if condensation was affecting your windows?**

Ans. (a) Drive for a few miles with a window open.
(b) Wipe the glass with the back of your hand.
* (c) Firstly, dry with a cloth and switch on the demister system.

Q. You may ensure visibility to the side and rear of the vehicle by ......

Ans.   (a)   using your rear view mirror.
    *   (b)   making full use of exterior mirrors.
       (c)   putting your head out the driver's window and looking behind.

Q. How could a high mounted cab affect your visibility?

Ans.   (a)   It could make it easier to see pedestrians and cyclists close up.
    *   (b)   It could make it more difficult to see pedestrians and cyclists close up.
       (c)   It could make it easier to drive in wet weather.

Q. To see the blind area to the front or side of a high mounted cab, you should .....

Ans. *   (a)   angle a mirror towards the blind area.
       (b)   ensure that the rear mirrors are angled directly to the rear.
       (c)   ensure that the mirrors are angled to show the body of the vehicle.

SAFETY OF VEHICLE LOADING AND PERSONS CARRIED

Q.   When delivering or collecting passengers or goods you should .....

Ans.   (a)   drive up on the footpath in order to minimise obstruction to other traffic.

     (b)   park on a corner provided the hazard warning lights are switched on.

 * (c)   avoid causing obstruction to other road users.

Q.   How could overloading affect your vehicle?

Ans.   (a)   It could cause the clutch to slip, rendering the vehicle immobile.

 * (b)   Its stability could be affected.

     (c)   The air filter could become clogged.

GETTING OUT FROM THE VEHICLE

Q.   What precautions should you take to secure the vehicle before getting out of it?

Ans.   (a)   Ensure that there is an adequate supply of air in the air-tanks.

     (b)   Ensure that the turbo-charger has cooled down.

 * (c)   Ensure that the hand-brake is on, that the ignition is switched off, and that a low gear is engaged.

Q. **What precautions should you take before getting out of the vehicle?**

Ans. (a) Leave the engine running with the parking brake 'on'.

(b) Switch off the engine and make sure the gear is in neutral.

* (c) Switch off the engine, apply the hand brake and engage a low gear.

Q. **Having parked your vehicle, what should you do before getting out of it?**

Ans. (a) Open the door and look around for oncoming traffic.

* (b) Look around and check your rear view mirrors for oncoming traffic before opening the door.

(c) Check your inside rear view mirror before opening the door.

Q. **What precaution should you take when allowing passengers to get out of your bus or minibus?**

Ans. * (a) Ensure that they get out on the side nearest to a footpath, where possible.

(b) Ensure that the bus is in a speed limit area.

(c) Watch for traffic in your rear-view mirrors and advise them when to get out.

ACCIDENTS

Q. How should following traffic be warned in the event of an accident?

Ans. * (a) Place the red reflectorised triangle on the road a short distance back from your vehicle.

(b) Switch on the vehicle's left hand indicator.

(c) Have a passenger or passer-by wave them down.

Q. In what circumstances would you use the emergency red reflectorised triangle?

Ans. (a) When loading or unloading.

(b) When reversing on a main road.

* (c) When an accident or breakdown occurs.

ENVIRONMENTAL MATTERS

Q. To avoid excessive exhaust pollution from your vehicle you should .....

Ans. (a) drive at higher speeds than normal in order to reduce the time spent on the road.

(b) use a fuel additive to increase the fuel octane rating.

* (c) change your vehicle's air filters regularly.

Q.   **Fuel efficiency is improved by .....**

Ans.   (a)   accelerating hard up through the gears to reach the desired speed as quickly as possible.

(b)   driving the vehicle in lower gear for as long as possible before changing up.

*   (c)   using gentle acceleration and making gear changes as recommended by the manufacturer's specification.

Part II

CATEGORY C

NECESSARY DOCUMENTS

Q.   To drive a vehicle with a maximum design gross vehicle weight of 7,500 kgs. you must hold a licence in which of the following categories?

       (a)   Category W.
       (b)   Category A1.
  * (c)   Category C1 or C.

Q.   What is the maximum design gross vehicle weight which the holder of a category C1 licence may drive?

Ans.   (a)   6,500 kg.
  * (b)   7,500 kg.
       (c)   8,500 kg.

Q.   Is the holder of a category C1 licence entitled to tow a trailer?

Ans. * (a)   Yes, up to 750 kg. gross vehicle weight.
       (b)   Yes, up to 1,000 kg. gross vehicle weight.
       (c)   No.

Q.   The maximum number of passengers that can be carried by the holder of a category C or C1 licence is .....

Ans.
    (a)   10.
    (b)   6.
* (c)   8.

Q.   What vehicles are required to have a Certificate of Roadworthiness issued every year?

Ans.
    (a)   All vehicles exceeding 1.5 tonnes g.v.w.
    (b)   All vehicles exceeding 2.5 tonnes g.v.w.
* (c)   All vehicles exceeding 3.5 tonnes g.v.w.

Q.   The plated weight of a vehicle is .....

Ans. * (a)   the maximum weight at which it is allowed to be driven.
    (b)   the unladen weight of the vehicle excluding fuel, tools and accessories.
    (c)   the gross vehicle weight of the vehicle less the unladen weight.

SPEED LIMIT

Q.   The maximum permitted speed for a truck
is .....

Ans.   (a)   45 m.p.h.
    * (b)   50 m.p.h.
     (c)   55 m.p.h.

Q.   The maximum permitted speed for a truck
on a motorway is .....

Ans.   (a)   70 m.p.h.
     (b)   60 m.p.h.
    * (c)   50 m.p.h.

VEHICLE WEIGHTS AND DIMENSIONS

Q.   The maximum permitted design gross
weight of a 4 axle rigid truck with
conventional (non air) suspension is .....

Ans.   (a)   20,500 kg.
    * (b)   30,500 kg.
     (c)   40,500 kg.

Q. The maximum permitted laden weight of a 4 axle rigid truck with road friendly (air) suspension is .....

Ans.   (a)   22,000 kg.
     *   (b)   32,000 kg.
         (c)   42,000 kg.

Q. The maximum permitted laden weight of a 3 axle rigid truck is .....

Ans. * (a)   26,000 kg.
         (b)   30,000 kg.
         (c)   32,000 kg.

Q. The maximum permitted laden weight of a 2 axle rigid truck with conventional suspension is .....

Ans.   (a)   15,000 kg.
     *   (b)   17,000 kg.
         (c)   20,000 kg.

Q. The maximum permitted laden weight of a 2 axle rigid truck with road friendly (air) suspension is .....

Ans.   (a)   15,000 kg.
     *   (b)   17,000 kg.
         (c)   20,000 kg.

BRAKING SYSTEMS

Q. What trucks are required to have a speed limiter fitted?

Ans. (a) Trucks with a design gross vehicle weight exceeding 10,000 kg.
* (b) Trucks with a design gross vehicle weight exceeding 12,000 kg.
(c) Trucks with a design gross vehicle weight exceeding 15,000 kg.

Q. What is the maximum speed limiter setting for heavy goods vehicles?

Ans. (a) 90 K.P.H.
* (b) 85 K.P.H.
(c) 80 K.P.H.

Q. The design gross vehicle weight above which trucks must be fitted with speed limiter is .....

Ans. * (a) 12,000 kg.
(b) 15,000 kg.
(c) 18,000 kg.

TECHNICAL MATTERS, WITH A BEARING ON ROAD SAFETY

Q. A warning buzzer in the cab usually indicates .....

Ans. (a) the lights have been left switched on.
   * (b) low air pressure in the braking system.
   (c) low fuel level.

Q. After driving over rough or broken ground you should check that .....

Ans. * (a) stones are not jammed between the rear double-wheels.
   (b) the tachometer does not show in the 'red.'
   (c) the weight limits are not exceeded for more than a half mile.

Q. A 'range change' gearbox allows the driver to .....

Ans. (a) choose between manual and semi-automatic transmission.
   (b) pre-select a gear for a particular purpose.
   * (c) select a series of either high or low ratio gears depending on the load being carried and/or the terrain.

Q. A two-speed axle .....

Ans. * (a) doubles the number of gear ratios available to a driver.
(b) holds the drive-axle at a particular speed when the vehicle is heavily laden.
(c) allows the driving wheels at the rear of the truck to rotate at different speeds.

Q. An 'unloader valve' .....

Ans. (a) operates the tailboard platform to facilitate unloading.
* (b) releases excess air pressure in the braking system.
(c) permits tipper bodies to be raised or lowered.

SAFETY OF VEHICLE LOADING

Q. Your truck may exceed its maximum permitted weight .....

Ans. (a) when the load cannot be divided up.
* (b) only when you have a special permit from the Garda Síochána for a particular load.
(c) on local journeys provided the Garda Síochána have been notified.

Q. How might an unevenly distributed load affect a truck?

Ans.   (a)   Overall fuel consumption is improved.
*   (b)   The truck's stability is adversely affected.
     (c)   Gears are more difficult to change.

Q. What effect would sharp braking have on a loosely secured load?

Ans.   (a)   The load would tend to go to the rear of the vehicle.
*   (b)   The load would tend to go to the front of the vehicle.
     (c)   The load would remain stable.

Q. What effect does a load have on your vehicle's braking ability?

Ans. * (a)   It increases the normal stopping distance required.
     (b)   It reduces the normal stopping distance required.
     (c)   It has no effect provided the brakes are in good condition.

Q. How does air-suspension affect a vehicle's carrying capacity compared to conventional suspension?

Ans. * (a) It allows extra weight to be carried.
(b) It requires less weight to be carried.
(c) It makes no difference.

Q. What additional precautions should be taken when transporting bulk liquid?

Ans. * (a) The tanks should be sectioned off.
(b) Tyre pressures should be increased.
(c) Short sharp braking movements should be used to bring the vehicle to a halt.

Q. How should a load of loose dusty material be carried?

Ans. * (a) It should be covered with a tarpaulin or sheeting.
(b) Uncovered.
(c) It should be dampened down with a water-hose.

Q.   When carrying hazardous materials, you should ensure that .....

Ans.   (a)   when in built up areas, you drive only at night.
            (b)   you have a telephone in the vehicle.
        *   (c)   you comply with the regulations on the conveyance of dangerous substances by road.

Q.   When carrying out an inspection under a raised tipper body, you should .....

Ans.   (a)   ensure that the body is raised to its full extent.
            (b)   ensure that the hydraulic oil reservoir is full.
        *   (c)   ensure that the body is supported by props.

Q.   When tipping a load from your vehicle you should .....

Ans.   * (a)   be aware of overhead cables.
            (b)   engage the tipping mechanism before opening the tail-gate.
            (c)   drive forward for a distance in order to ensure complete discharge of the load.

Q.   Must a rear-load overhang which exceeds I metre be marked by a red flag or marker?

Ans.   (a)   No.
        *   (b)   Yes.
            (c)   Yes but only at night.

Q.   **The maximum weight which an axle is designed to carry .....**

Ans.   *   (a)   may not be exceeded.
                (b)   may be exceeded on journeys of less than 50 miles.
                (c)   may be exceeded on motorways only.

Q.   **A lifting axle .....**

Ans.   (a)   enables the vehicle body to be raised or lowered when loading or unloading.
                (b)   is coupled to a power take-off unit which operates an accessory such as a crane or winch.
        *   (c)   may be raised or lowered depending on the load being carried.

Q.   **What is the difference in handling between a short and long wheelbase truck?**

Ans.   *   (a)   Short wheelbase vehicles are less stable at high speed.
                (b)   Short wheelbase vehicles are more stable at high speed.
                (c)   Short wheelbase vehicles need more room to turn.

VEHICLE SAFETY EQUIPMENT

Q.   **What colour rear markings must be fitted to a category 'C' type vehicle?**

Ans.   *   (a)   Red fluorescent and red reflectorised stripes.

             (b)   Black and amber reflectorised stripes.

             (c)   Red and amber reflectorised stripes.

Q.   **What is the purpose of rear under-run barriers?**

Ans.   *   (a)   To prevent cars or light goods vehicles from going under the body of the vehicle from the rear.

             (b)   To facilitate access to the side and rear doors.

             (c)   To prevent the theft of the spare wheel and tools.

GETTING OUT FROM THE VEHICLE

Q.   **How should a driver get out of a truck cab?**

Ans.   (a)   Jump clearly to the ground.

             (b)   Use the steps and hand-rails provided while facing away from the cab.

       *   (c)   Use the steps and hand-rails provided while facing towards the cab.

ENVIRONMENTAL MATTERS

Q.   When leaving a construction site or quarry, you should ensure that .....

Ans.   (a)   the retarder is engaged.

*   (b)   the wheels and mudguards are not covered with mud and debris.

(c)   the diff-lock is engaged.

PART III

CATEGORY D

NECESSARY DOCUMENTS

Q. Is the holder of a category D or D1 provisional licence allowed to carry passengers for hire or reward while driving a bus?

Ans.   (a)   Yes.

     *   (b)   No.

         (c)   Yes, if accompanied by a full category D licence holder.

Q. A Public Service Vehicle licence is required .....

Ans. *   (a)   when driving a vehicle which is carrying passengers for reward.

         (b)   only if driving a school bus.

         (c)   only if driving a taxi or hackney-cab.

Q. A Road Passenger Certificate must be held by .....

Ans,   (a)   a bus or coach driver.

     *   (b)   a person or firm with a business involved in the transporting by road of persons for reward.

         (c)   a passenger on a bus who is entitled to free travel.

SPEED LIMIT

Q. What is the maximum speed limit of a single deck bus or minibus with standing passengers?

Ans. * (a) 40 m.p.h.
 (b) 50 m.p.h.
 (c) 45 m.p.h.

Q. What is the maximum speed limit of a single deck bus or minibus not carrying standing passengers?

Ans. (a) 40 m.p.h.
 * (b) 50 m.p.h.
 (c) 45 m.p.h.

Q. What is the maximum speed limit of a double-decker bus?

Ans. (a) 30 m.p.h.
 * (b) 40 m.p.h.
 (c) 50 m.p.h.

VEHICLE WEIGHTS AND DIMENSIONS

Q. The maximum permitted weight of a two-axled bus is .....

Ans. * (a) 17,000 kg.
 (b) 18,000 kg.
 (c) 19,000 kg.

Q. The maximum permitted width of a bus is .....

Ans. (a) 5 feet, two and a half inches.
(b) 7 feet, two and a half inches.
* (c) 8 feet, two and a half inches.

Q. The maximum permitted height of a double-decker bus is .....

Ans. * (a) 4.57 metres.
(b) 5.57 metres.
(c) 6.57 metres.

BRAKING SYSTEMS

Q. What is the maximum speed governor setting for buses?

Ans. * (a) 100 K.P.H. (62 m.p.h.).
(b) 120 K.P.H. (75 m.p.h.).
(c) 80 K.P.H. (50 m.p.h.)

Q. What is the minimum gross vehicle weight above which buses must be fitted with a speed governor?

Ans. * (a) 10,000 kg.
(b) 12,000 kg.
(c) 8,000 kg.

Q. **What buses are required to have a speed limiter fitted?**

Ans. (a) Buses with more than 16 passenger seats.
(b) Buses with more than 30 passenger seats.
* (c) Buses with more than 8 passenger seats and a laden weight of more than 10,000 kg.

WEATHER RELATED MATTERS

Q. **What effect could strong cross-wind have on a double-decker bus?**

Ans. * (a) It could make it more liable to turn over.
(b) It could reduce braking time.
(c) It could increase braking time.

CARRYING PASSENGERS

Q. **How many passengers may you carry on your bus?**

Ans. * (a) As many as your PSV license allows you.
(b) As many as there are seats available.
(c) As many as can fit in without a crush.

Q. **What is the maximum number of adult passengers which a D1 licence entitles you to carry in your minibus?**

Ans. (a) 14.
* (b) 16.
(c) 18.

Q. What is the maximum number of child passengers which a category D1 licence entitles you to carry in your minibus?

Ans. (a) 16.
     (b) 20.
   * (c) 24.

Q. When carrying children, should the passenger doors be locked?

Ans. * (a) Yes, in case a child would open one while the bus is moving.
     (b) No, in order to facilitate easy entry and exit from the bus or minibus.
     (c) Not in urban areas, or where frequent pick up points are located.

SAFETY OF VEHICLE LOADING

Q. Where should passengers' luggage be stowed?

Ans. (a) In the passageway.
     (b) Behind the seats.
   * (c) In the luggage compartment and, if hand luggage, in the overhead rack.

VEHICLE SAFETY EQUIPMENT

Q. Which of the following items should be carried on your bus or minibus?

Ans. * (a) Fire extinguisher, first aid kit and red warning triangle.

(b) Fire extinguisher, fan, and public address system.

(c) First aid kit and public address system.

GETTING OUT FROM THE VEHICLE

Q. When should the passengers' door be opened on your bus or minibus?

Ans. (a) When travelling in a built up area at low speeds.

(b) When within 50 metres of a bus stop.

* (c) Only when stopped at a safe place for passengers to get out.

Q When you wish to stop to allow passengers to get off your bus, you should .....

Ans. (a) stop as close as possible to a junction.

* (b) stop where they will not be in danger from other traffic.

(c) pull up on the footpath.

ACCIDENTS

Q. In the event of an accident where fuel has spilled on to the road, and nobody is injured, you should .....

Ans. (a) dilute the fuel with water from the radiator if necessary.

* (b) get the passengers to a safe area as quickly as possible.

(c) switch on the hazard warning lights and warn passengers not to smoke.

Q. Where your bus or minibus is broken down in the middle of the road following an accident, you should .....

Ans. (a) warn your passengers to sit still until help arrives.

(b) advise your passengers when it is safe for them to make a dash to the pavement or roadside.

* (c) guide each passenger individually to the pavement or roadside.

Q. If your bus or minibus is involved in an accident, which of these should you do first?

Ans. * (a) Ensure that your passengers are guided to safety.

(b) Confine your passengers to their seats.

(c) Look for witnesses among your passengers.